Beyond The Canon's Plays for Young Activists

Beyond The Canon's Plays for Young Activists

Three Plays by Women from the Global Majority

Muhammad Ali and Me

A Museum in Baghdad

Acceptance

Edited by

SIMEILIA HODGE-DALLAWAY *and* SARUDZAYI MARUFU

methuen | drama

LONDON • NEW YORK • OXFORD • NEW DELHI • SYDNEY

METHUEN DRAMA
Bloomsbury Publishing Plc
50 Bedford Square, London, WC1B 3DP, UK
1385 Broadway, New York, NY 10018, USA
29 Earlsfort Terrace, Dublin 2, Ireland

BLOOMSBURY, METHUEN DRAMA and the Methuen Drama logo are trademarks
of Bloomsbury Publishing Plc

First published in Great Britain 2023

Cover design by Rebecca Heselton.
Cover image: *Lady with the Braid*, Oscar Ukonu, 2020, Ballpoint pen on paper, 55 × 71 cm

A catalogue record for this book is available from the British Library.

A catalog record for this book is available from the Library of Congress.

ISBN: PB: 978-1-3502-9499-8
        ePDF: 978-1-3502-9500-1
        eBook: 978-1-3502-9501-8

Series: Methuen Drama Plays Collections

Typeset by RefineCatch Limited, Bungay, Suffolk
Printed and bound in Great Britain

To find out more about our authors and books visit www.bloomsbury.com
and sign up for our newsletters.

This book is dedicated to Simeilia Hodge-Dallaway's twin warriors Reign London McKamie and Royal Cali McKamie.

Simeilia and Sarudzayi extend the dedication of this book to their greatest inspirations, their mothers Charmaine Miller and Agnes Zirobwa and to the many Black and Global Majority women who will forever be the Ultimate Champions of Activism.

Contents

Access additional materials and resources on the Beyond The Canon
Companion Website: bloomsbury.pub/BeyondTheCanon

Acknowledgement

We gratefully acknowledge financial assistance from the Arts Council England and the National Lottery.

Beyond The Canon is an organisation committed to increase the visibility and accessibility of ground-breaking yet lesser-known classics, masterpieces and gems by British and international culturally diverse playwrights.

Working in collaboration with theatres, academia and publishing houses, Beyond The Canon produces UK and international revivals, monologue showcases, workshops, publications and podcasts. Founded and led by Simeilia Hodge-Dallaway with executive producer Sarudzayi Marufu, Beyond The Canon aims to support, empower and inspire culturally diverse artists, and enrich the artistic industry in the UK and across the world.

www.beyondthecanon.com @beyondthecanon

Introduction by Simeilia Hodge-Dallaway

Dear Young Activists,

I truly believe that plays have the ability to be the most powerful tool in the world, depending on whose hands and ears they fall upon. It is no secret that the arts have an unbeatable universal track-record to influence and change policies, bring greater awareness of social injustices and, more importantly, it forces us to acknowledge our own privilege and agency so that we can create the change we want to see in our lives and in the world.

As an activist, I have always had a profound respect for writers of politically charged plays, because they go the distance to boldly take the road less travelled which is usually risky, univiting and challenging territory for altruistic reasons. These writers, truth-seekers and sharers, have a unique gift of making some of the most complex issues accessible, personal and yet also engaging and entertaining. We are able to understand long-standing political and economic battles between and within countries across the world, deep-rooted cross-generational racial issues within communities, and enter the hearts and minds of our beloved heroes and leaders.

I chose the arts as a career because I recognized the power of theatre and storytelling. Like many people, I have watched or read a play and have been inspired to take action: create a company, produce and direct plays, donate to a charity, book a trip to a different part of the world to meet and work with a specific community, protest in solidarity for a cause or educate my family and local community on issues and new ways of thinking about a subject matter or community. I love the fact that after watching or reading a play, we are able to participate in energetically charged and informed conversations with family, friends and strangers, debating character motives, casting strong opinions about the actions they took and even seeing ourselves in stories that could not be further away from our realities.

Every time we encounter these plays we walk away with a greater connection with the people in the world. It is for this reason that I founded my company Beyond The Canon and decided to edit this book with my fellow activist and Beyond The Canon producer, Sarudzayi Marufu.

Beyond The Canon exists to shine a light on past and present plays written by writers of colour (the global majority) who aspire to change the world. It is deliberate in its efforts to make the world more aware of theatre-activists that exist within our rich legacy who have used their talents to educate and influence the world for the better and to inspire more politically conscious artists to repeat the cycle.

For Beyond The Canon's first publication, we have selected three groundbreaking plays from some of my favourite inspirational kick-ass female playwrights of colour: Mojisola Adebayo, Hannah Khalil and Amy Ng. It was difficult to choose one play from each of their extensive catalogues to feature in this book, because all of their plays are equally powerful, relevant and extraordinary. Therefore, after reading the plays featured in this book, I encourage you all to take the time to read more plays written by these incredible writers.

It is an absolute honour to feature the plays *Muhammad Ali and Me* by Mojisola Adebayo, *A Museum in Baghdad* by Hannah Khalil and *Acceptance* by Amy Ng. All three plays have the ability to remain with you long after reading them and I am confident that you will be compelled to study, share and perform them – and, like me, be inspired to create your own form of activism.

What makes this book even more special is the insertion of our bespoke Beyond The Canon commissioned learning resources carefully constructed for each play featured in this collection by theatre and education professionals: Reginald Edmund, Chris White and Amy Ng. This added feature provides you with exclusive insight into the creation of the play, the playwright's creative journey, provocations and practical challenges to deepen your understanding of the play and take your activism to new heights.

The learning resources found in this book are supported by a companion website which features scene-by-scene breakdowns, historical overview to the world of the play, drama exercises, and audio and visual material.

Now that you have your hands on our first Beyond The Canon Plays for Young Activists anthology, you will never read a play in the same way again.

As young activists, these bespoke resources are your golden ticket to unlock the ultimate activist in you!

Introduction by Sarudzayi Marufu

Dear Young Activist,

I too am an activist. This is not bragging or fighting talk, but simply a fact. For the longest time, I did not believe myself to be someone worthy of carrying a title so heavy. Such was meant for the great shoulders of James Baldwin, Maya Angelou, Marsha P. Johnson, Nelson Mandela, Mbuya Nehanda and Olive Morris – to name a few. A special breed of person that seemed destined to live an extraordinary life and to be remembered for their legendary deeds.

I did not become like them to be the activist I am. Instead, I became better informed. Whilst I was still inspired by the legends, I also gained inspiration from the greatness of those nearer to me. As I learned more and as I grew from that knowledge, I witnessed how the numerous artists whose work moved me and made me feel seen was their activism. I became aware of my legacy and gained strength from it. Realising the richness in the culture available to me and seeking out what was unknown to me, hidden from me and doing so with joy for it added value to my journey to know that I was continuing the work of those who came before me.

I began to truly understand that it was not the word 'activism' that was too heavy, but more myself who did not realise the strength within my shoulders. I no longer felt alone in my attempts; I felt supported by the strength of others.

With this book, Simeilia and I have collated the work of three incredible artists. Their activism should be accessible to all. We have endeavoured to play a small part in your comprehension of their art, and their intention. We have done so from a place of admiration and a desire to impart our brand of activism. I am forever inspired by Mojisola Adebayo, Hannah Khalil, Amy Ng and Simeilia Hodge-Dallaway. Like so many others, these women have enriched my life, helping me understand what it means to be my kind of activist. I am also grateful to Reginald Edmund, Chris White and of course Amy Ng, for exploring their connection to these 3 plays and sharing their comprehension with us.

I hope that, as you journey through this book and supporting website, you will further awaken within you your agency. That you will reassess your journey, see the value in your actions to this moment, draw strength from your legacy and your knowledge of it, and grow bolder in your determination to make an impact on the world moving forward.

You are an activist. When you know this, you realise that your activism is limitless.

Beyond The Canon's top tips for creating a safe space

We all know how it feels to be in an unsafe space where our needs have not been considered, but how do we create a safe space for everyone?

The dictionary defines a safe space as 'a place or environment in which a person or category of people can feel confident that they will not be exposed to discrimination, criticism, harassment or another emotional or physical harm'.

Creating a safe space is a form of activism.

Working within a safe space is essential to the work that we do at Beyond The Canon. Our mission is to encourage everyone to take a deeper unapologetic dive into who they are, incite curiosity of cultural experiences and worldly perspectives and exercise their arts activism.

This can only be achieved in a supportive, trusted and respected environment.

Here are our ten tips for creating a safe space which we have designed inspired by carrying out our work at Beyond The Canon.

1. *The physical space:*
   a. Each space should consist of two elements. The room which you work out of and a safe zone – a separate space where participants can excuse themselves should they require a moment to collect their thoughts.
   b. A counsellor or advisor can be present in the safe zone (optional).

2. *Inclusive and diverse facilitators/teams:*
   a. An inclusive space with a team of diverse facilitators is always safest. It allows for more clear and open discussions.
   b. We encourage you to bring in experts or individuals with relevant personal experience.

3. *Ensure to check in and check out at the beginning of each session:*
   a. Everyone walks into the space from a different place, be it physically or emotionally. It is important to start with a reset and a regroup.
   b. Checking out is essential to closing out each secession. It is imperative to shake out the work and get back to self. Always end the work with gratitude to everyone in the space.

4. *Time-out:*
   a. Do not be afraid to take a time-out. It may be the most useful tool you have.
   b. Frequent breaks are also a good alternative.

5. *Escalation:*
   a. Ensure that there is a clear and communicated escalation protocol. Participants should know that they have someone outside the space they can reach out to, should they need to.
   b. Spaces should be reassessed and reviewed regularly to ensure effectiveness.

6. *Time:*

   a. It is important to have enough time. Being time poor can lead to improper check-ins and check-outs, discussions being rushed, and participants leaving the space discontent and unsure.

7. *Language:*

   a. It is the role of the facilitator to ensure that the language used is understandable, accessible and inclusive.

8. *Confidentiality:*

   a. Everything discussed should be confidential. This will allow for freer and more open discussion.

   b. There should be a clause communicated to all participants that disconcerting or harmful revelations will not be protected under the confidentiality clause.

9. *Transparency:*

   a. Always ensure transparency in all matters. Clear communication will aid with ensuring that no participants are left blindsided.

   b. Be clear about who is in the space and what purpose they serve.

10. *Personal not general:*

    a. All participants should contribute from a personal perspective rather than a general one. Everyone should meet on an equal footing and self-nomination should be practised.

Be fierce, be bold and be free to deep dive into this work.

How to become the ultimate activist

Congratulations – you have taken the first step to becoming the ultimate activist.

This book is your personal guide to elevate your activism and bring sustainable change to the world. To help you along the way, here are Beyond The Canon's **FOUR CHAMPIONS OF ACTIVISM**.

Which activist are you?

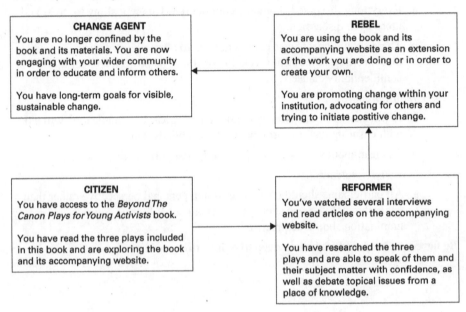

CHANGE AGENT
You are no longer confined by the book and its materials. You are now engaging with your wider community in order to educate and inform others.

You have long-term goals for visible, sustainable change.

REBEL
You are using the book and its accompanying website as an extension of the work you are doing or in order to create your own.

You are promoting change within your institution, advocating for others and trying to initiate postitive change.

CITIZEN
You have access to the *Beyond The Canon Plays for Young Activists* book.

You have read the three plays included in this book and are exploring the book and its accompanying website.

REFORMER
You've watched several interviews and read articles on the accompanying website.

You have researched the three plays and are able to speak of them and their subject matter with confidence, as well as debate topical issues from a place of knowledge.

Keep an eye out

Throughout the book we will offer provocations that are linked to each of the champions of activism. These provocations are perfect for classroom debates, group discussions and personal reflection. We encourage you to explore all the tiers and have fun transitioning into the ultimate activist: THE CHANGE AGENT!

Muhammad Ali and Me

Mojisola Adebayo

MOJISOLA ADEBAYO
PLAYS ONE
INTRODUCTION BY LYNETTE GODDARD

MOJ OF THE ANTARCTIC: AN AFRICAN ODYSSEY
MUHAMMAD ALI AND ME
DESERT BOY
MATT HENSON, NORTH STAR

Playwright's introduction: Mojisola Adebayo

Thank you for reading *Muhammad Ali and Me!*

I never dreamed the play would be read so widely. I really just wrote the script because I needed it, for my own learning, growth and healing so it is a dream come true that the play could in some small way be useful for other people too. The play began as a short performance-making project as part of my own studies on an MA programme. I was researching the ways in which Black peoples of the African diaspora have historically used performance skills in everyday life as part of our liberation. Muhammad Ali struck me as one such important figure – dancing in the boxing ring, rapping at press conferences, magic tricks on the streets – he knew the power of performance in playing with perceptions and unpacking prejudice. I'd often had to perform my way out of oppressive situations too, whether it be making my parents laugh (instead of fight) while I did accents and silly impressions as a child or, later in life, pretending to be a man when I was followed home by a predator. Theatre has been my saviour, both on the stage and off it. However, when I first wrote the script it was only about Ali (not me) and a friend asked, 'Where are you in all this?' I had not imagined that anything inspired by my own story could be interesting but I began to experiment with the idea of a character, loosely based on my own childhood, who could be in some kind of fantastical friendship with Ali. It worked and the rest is in the play! Ali showed us that we can all be champions in our lives, we can all be protagonists, no one else has the right to dictate or narrate who we can be. Moreover, Ali showed me that my small life is part of many lives, part of a tremendous Black history and Black future. We can, and do, defeat abusers, predators and oppressors. We tell our own stories in our own ways, we fly on butterflies and bees, we float and sting and lose and get up again and, collectively, we win, win, win. This play is for everybody and that means those who have been most excluded, including people who are D/deaf, visually or physically impaired. Ali spent most of his life as a (so-called) disabled person and that reminds me that able-bodiedness is only ever temporary. So, that's why the interpretation into Sign Language is also very important and I hope you find ways of exploring access in your thinking with the play too. I hope it inspires you to make your own work, in whatever form that gives you pleasure, and to use your limited time on this planet to help end racism, disability discrimination, sexism, homophobia, Islamophobia and their horrible legacies. Everything could be and can be different – change begins in your imagination and by putting yourself in the place of another person.

Courage to you and *ubuntu*!

A physical storytelling performance for three performers, with poetry, song, dance, British (or other) Sign Language, ritual, music and movement, animation, original fight footage, film and verbatim text by Muhammad Ali.

Muhammad Ali and Me is dedicated to Muhammad Ali and is offered in memory of Emmett Till.
Their stories are shared within this play.

Muhammad Ali and Me was created by the Ali Collective and was first performed at Ovalhouse on 11 November 2008.

The Ali Collective

Writer/Producer/Performer playing Mojitola and Muhammad Ali	Mojisola Adebayo
Performer – Corner Man	Charlie Folorunsho
British Sign Language Performer – Referee	Jacqui Beckford
Director and Choreographer	Sheron Wray
Designer	Rajha Shakiry
Lighting Designer	Crin Claxton
Composer and Singing Coach	Juwon Ogungbe
Recorded Music Supervisor	Debo Adebayo
Visuals Editor	Sue Giovanni
Dramaturg	Amani Naphtali
Production/Stage Manager	Marijke Zwart
Audience Development Officer	Abidemi Mosaku
Boxing Trainer	Clinton Mckenzie
Magician/Tricks Consultant	Roy Davenport Magic

Special thanks to Stuart Pampellone for the original development of this work.

Performance notes – Roles

Mojitola begins the play as a girl of around five years old. She is a Black South Londoner, of mixed Nigerian (Yoruba) and Danish heritage. She is imaginative, excitable and afraid. **Muhammad Ali** is the boxing legend and political activist of the 1960s and 1970s who appears to **Mojitola** and befriends her. **Mojitola** and **Muhammad Ali** are both played by the same female physical actor and singer. The vocal and physical impersonation of Ali must be very accurate.

Corner Man is played by a versatile Black male physical actor and singer. His title denotes a 'persona' within which he animates stories and plays many characters including a **Boy** (a childhood friend); the **Daddy** who is also the **Griot** storyteller; **Mummy Angie** – **Mojitola**'s foster mother, **Jimmy** – **Mummy Angie**'s grown-up son; the wrestler **Gorgeous George**; **Malcolm X**; a **School Child** and **Teachers One** and **Two** (primary and secondary); **Angelo Dundee** and **Bundini** – Ali's trainers; the army **Doctor**; **Michelle** and **Donna** (secondary school bullies); various **Passers-By**; **Rahman** – Ali's brother; a **Lawyer**; **TV/Reporters**; **Police Officer**; the **Judge**; a university **Lecturer**; an acting **Tutor** and **Andreas** – an acting student; a protesting **Student**; a **Stage Manager**; the boxer **George Foreman** and his **Trainer**; and a **TV Floor Manager**. When he is not playing these characters, the performer returns to being **Corner Man**, indicated by stage positioning, physicality and a prop (such as a towel) if helpful.

Referee is played by a female physical performer and creative British Sign Language (BSL) interpreter. In theory **Referee** can be played by a female actor of any cultural heritage, but was originally cast as a Black woman. For clarity, only the words **Referee** voices aloud are noted. Unless otherwise stated, **Referee** communicates the whole text into British Sign Language. At times, the **Referee** interprets the scenes within the frame of a role such as a childhood friend, Mummy, the magician's glamorous assistant, various school children, a teacher, a court clerk, demonstrators, a lover, a television director, as indicated in the script and all through the languages of BSL, movement, dance, magic, song, etc.

Style of playing

- physical storytelling within a broadly African aesthetic, very influenced by the work of Denise Wong and Black Mime Theatre
- with use of ritual
- a capella singing
- dance of the African diaspora
- a fantastic 1970s vinyl soundtrack is crucial
- a sense of musicality throughout in speech as well as song
- interaction with visuals on multiple 1970s television screens
- minimal props and set – each object has a significance beyond its use
- accessible/inclusive

- with all actors on stage continually (with only a few exceptions)
- audience interaction

Set

The play is set within a fractured boxing gym, with elements of a boxing ring including canvas floor, ropes, bells, stools, heavy bag, speed bag, etc. The boxing ring posts are made of 1970s televisions on which the visuals are played. Thus the boxing framework is broken up stylistically by fragments of a 1970s working-class London home with armchair, pouf, telephone, child's single bed doubling as a changing-room bench and various props indicated in the script. The set also briefly becomes a street, school, playground, police station, court room, dressing room, TV set, etc. as indicated in the script. The audience are seated on two or four sides around the playing area.

A note on the 'truth' of this play

Muhammad Ali and Me is inspired by real life experiences. It is a subjective truth, which is not necessarily always based on fact. The play is in part *about* the merging of memory and imagination, biography and fiction.

Pre-Show

An eclectic mix of 1970s vinyl music, disco, reggae, funk, ska, punk . . . with lyrics relevant to themes in the show.

Scene One: Opening Ritual

Pre-show music fades out. Beginners music plays, something powerful, classy, awesome that builds up the boxing ring atmosphere and takes us to Black America, the diaspora . . . e.g. 'Also Sprach Zarathustra' by Deodato. **Referee** *leads the way in.* **Mojitola** *walks behind as a boxer in white dressing gown with hood up.* **Corner Man** *walks behind her. Dim light, follow spot on performers, smoke.* **Referee** *enters the ring and stands in the centre waiting to start the fight.* **Mojitola** *and* **Corner Man** *circle the exterior of the boxing ring, formed by the seating of the audience.* **Mojitola** *moves in a stylized slow shuffling-type movement in forward motion only, her feet do not leave the ground, her centre of gravity is low, her head and back are bent over at an approximately forty-five-degree angle, her eyes look at the floor, her shoulders are hunched, her arms are locked, her hands make fists.* **Corner Man** *walks slowly but upright. He makes a rhythmical movement with his white towel. Crossing it from one shoulder to the next. There is a sense of formality and seriousness about the proceedings. Coming through the music and soundscape and before the players enter the ring is a boxing announcer's voice, which could be spoken live by the* **Stage Manager**.

Announcer   Introducing . . . the Fighter, the Corner Man and the Referee –

Mojitola/Ali *and* **Corner Man** *enter the ring. Together with* **Referee**, *they carry out a series of precise choreographed ritual actions in an inward-facing triangle. The ritual involves removing and placing the robe, testing the ropes, prayer, passing a bottle of water, spitting a libation into the bucket, touching fists, etc.* **Corner Man** *hands* **Mojitola/Ali** *the skipping rope. She takes centre stage.* **Referee** *rings the bell.* **Mojitola** *stands poised with rope, ready to skip, then . . .*

Scene Two: Childhood in the 1970s

Mojitola (*speaking as* **Mojitola** *the grown-up woman*)
Muhammad Ali
And me
Have only one thing
In common.
We were Black, in the seventies.

(*Suddenly shifting energy and speaking as herself at five years old, bright colourful lighting.*) I AM THE GREATEST! (*She skips on two feet jumping and speaking simultaneously.*) I'm young! I'm handsome! I'm pretty! I'm fast! I can't possibly be beat! Two million dollars and change! Two million dollars and change! Change!

Mojitola *breaks into singing a medley of songs from the 1960s and 1970s. She uses the skipping rope handle as a microphone.* **Corner Man** *grabs the other end of the skipping rope handle and joins in singing songs.* **Corner Man** *and* **Referee** *play childhood friends all playing together.* **Referee** *signs all the lyrics in role.* **Corner Man** *plays* **Boy**.

Mojitola
Muhammad, Muhammad Ali, floats like a butterfly, stings like a bee![1]

Boy
I'm black and I'm proud![2]

Mojitola
Young gifted and –[3]

Boy
The ink is black.

Mojitola
The page is white.

Boy and Mojitola
Together we learn to read and write, to read and –[4]

Boy
Get on up! Stay on the scene!

Mojitola
Get on up!

Boy
Like a sex machine[5]

Mojitola *breaks into giggles.*

Boy and Mojitola (*impersonating* **Ali** *and his trainer* **Bundini**)
Aaaaaaah! Rumble, young man, rumble!

Mojitola *starts to go off on one, camping it up in a high-pitched voice, enjoying the gender play of the lyrics.*

Well, you can tell by the way I use my walk
I'm a woman's man,

[1] From 'Black Superman' by Johnny Wakelin and the Kinshasa Band, 1975.
[2] From 'Say It Loud – I'm Black and I'm Proud' by James Brown, 1968.
[3] From 'Young, Gifted and Black' by Nina Simone and Weldon Irvine, 1970.
[4] From 'Black and White' by David Arkin and Earl Robinson, 1956.
[5] From 'Sex Machine' by James Brown, 1970.

(Like a record jumping.)

>   I'm a woman's man,[6]
>   I'm a w-w-w-w –

Boy

>   – the revolution will not be televised!

Mojitola

>   The revolution will be live![7]

Boy

>   Until the philosophy which holds one race superior and another inferior is finally, and permanently, discredited, well everywhere is war . . .[8]

Mojitola

>   . . . I was born by the river,
>   In a little tent,
>   Oh and just like that river I've been running,
>   ever since,
>   It's been long,
>   A long time coming but I know,
>   A change gonna come,
>   Oh yes it will . . .[9]

'More Than a Woman' by Tavares plays, breaking the atmosphere.

Mojitola *screams with excitement.*

Mojitola Tuuuuune!

Mojitola *mimes the words of the song, as would a drag queen. She flirts with the audience. Pretends the skipping rope handle is a scarf, her hair, a willy, etc.* **Corner Man** *throws in the towel. The music stops suddenly.* **Corner Man** *now plays* **Daddy** *who has caught his daughter being rude. He is a stern, middle-aged man, speaks in a Nigerian (Yoruba) accent:*

Daddy MO-JI-TO-LA! (*'A Fifth of Beethoven' by Walter Murphy from the* Saturday Night Fever *album kicks in and plays under the text. It begins with the opening notes of Beethoven's fifth symphony and then switches to funk.* **Daddy***'s tone is also serious at first; he then switches to being lighter as the music changes to 1970s funk.*) What are you doing? Who are you?! You would be severely punished, if it wasn't your *birthday*! One, two, three, four, you are FIVE! (*He gives her a chopper bicycle. He sings a Nigerian-style 'Happy Birthday' along to the track.*) *Happy birthday to you, on this occasion of course, happy birthday to you, many happy returns . . .*

Mojitola *starts to ride the bike around the exterior of the ring, circling past the audience, interacting with them; she is very happy.* **Daddy** *is still singing.* **Mojitola**

---

[6] From 'Stayin' Alive' by the Bee Gees, 1977.
[7] From 'The Revolution Will Not Be Televised' by Gil Scott-Heron, 1970.
[8] From 'War' by Bob Marley, 1976 (directly quoting a speech made by Emperor Haile Selassie I in 1963).
[9] From 'A Change Is Gonna Come' by Sam Cooke, 1964.

jumps off the bicycle and starts chatting to an audience member, improvising.
Referee, *playing a child, takes the bike, rides it away and hides it out of view.*

Mojitola   Where's my bike? Someone's stolen my bike! (*Starts to cry.*) My daddy's gonna kill me. It's not fair! I want justice!

Corner Man   Then you better learn how to fight.

Mojitola (*to* **Referee**)   Referee! I need a referee! I need a mummy! . . .

Mojitola *directs the word 'mummy' to* **Referee**. *The music rewinds, indicating a flashback.*

Scene Three: The Family Home – A Flashback

Music. Possibly 'Slipping' into Darkness' by War. A fight/movement sequence without words ensues which demonstrates domestic violence. **Corner Man** *plays* **Daddy**, *beating* **Mummy**, *who is played by* **Referee**. **Daddy** *hits the punch bag as if it was his wife.* **Mummy** *reacts as if she is being hit, behind* **Mojitola** *who is curled up in the armchair, shaking from shock.* **Mojitola***'s shaking and freezing is a movement motif which will recur throughout the play.* **Daddy** *punches the bag whilst he speaks.*

Daddy   She doesn't love us. She doesn't love you. She doesn't love me. I told her. I told her. You will never ever take my child away from me. My blood. You will never see her again. Believe. You can only trust my blood. I am your father. Forget her. You never knew her. I am your father . . .

Mojitola *is increasingly traumatized by what she sees. The shaking and the violence culminates in* **Mojitola** *freezing, in a catatonic state.* **Mummy** *kisses* **Mojitola** *on the forehead and exits the ring; she remains frozen. The music fades out.* **Referee** *returns to playing the interpreter.* **Daddy** *speaks hypnotically, bringing* **Mojitola** *out of her trance.*

Daddy   . . . I am a professional. I am an accountant. I come from a long line of educated people. She was nothing. Zero. One . . . Two . . . Three . . . Four . . . you are FIVE!

Daddy *indicates the chopper bike, which has reappeared.*

Mojitola   My bike!

End of flashback. 'A Fifth of Beethoven' winds forward again, indicating we are returning to present time. **Mojitola** *is happy she has the bike back. She rides the bike around the exterior of the ring again, like before.* **Corner Man** *as* **Daddy** *hears the phone ring. He takes the phone. He is visibly shocked by bad news. We do not hear the conversation as the music is playing over it. Has to sit on his stool. He puts the phone down. Music fades down. He calls.*

Daddy   MO-JI-TO-LA!

Mojitola (*calling up to him*)   Daddy, I did my sums already, it was just a little bit hard! . . . (*She is consumed with her bike.*)

Daddy   Mojitola! Come along!

Mojitola   Aaaw . . . is it time to pray now?!

Daddy   Ah-ah! (*A telling-off.*)

Mojitola *reluctantly goes inside with her bike.*

Mojitola   Is it time for prayers?

Daddy   You do not shout about prayer in front of the whole of Colchester Court. Do you understand?

Mojitola (*doesn't understand*)   Yes, Daddy, not really.

Daddy   Be seated.

Mojitola *sits.* **Daddy** *stands. He addresses the child with the following speech with a certain pained formality while trying to keep emotional control. His pain grows during the speech as he realizes his small family is broken.*

Daddy   There are rumours of war. Home is calling me. You are no longer a little baby. You will be starting school in September. You know your ABC. You count. I have seen you can multiply. You will eventually divide. I am satisfied I have made good progress with you, despite all of the . . . distractions. From now on England will provide. She will be your mother. You will receive the best education in the world. As for time outside of school, I have appointed an English lady to be responsible for your welfare. Mrs Groom. Many of our people place their children with Angela Groom, when the hostels do not allow them rooms. In all probability there will be many African children like you there. We are often faced with few alternatives in this life. My father too had his own struggles. But step by step, by the grace of God, we do our best. (*He looks at her during the following.*) I have invested a substantial sum in Mrs Groom. So as we step to the door tomorrow morning, do not cry. If you cry, you will be severely punished. Do you understand? (**Mojitola** *shakes her head.*) Remember *who you are*. Act, always, as a good girl. Eat no pork. Study hard. Stay away from boys.

Mojitola   Yes, Daddy. (*Beat.*) When are you coming back?

Daddy   At the right time. God willing. (*Small pause.*)

Mojitola   Daddy, when?

Daddy   Be upstanding for scripture.

Daddy *indicates 'Get the Bible'.* **Mojitola** *gets the large book, upset, trying to make sense of it.*

Mojitola   Daddy . . . Is it a *story*?

Small pause.

Daddy (*with rare tenderness*)   No, my daughter. It is not a story.

They read from the Old Testament book of Ecclesiastes. Family photos from the 1970s are projected. As he reads he is battling with intense emotions. He is immensely sad to leave his daughter. Deeply afraid of what is to come, full of anxiety and uncertainty. **Mojitola** *is processing this transition. It is a rite of passage for her. The scene becomes ritual-like, a handing over from the father to the child. There is simple movement. A change of their standing positions, like two hands on a clock.*

Daddy
For every thing there is a season, and a time to every action under heaven:

Daddy/Mojitola
a time to be born, and a time to die;
a time to plant, and a time to uproot;
a time to kill, and a time to heal;
a time to break down, and a time to build up;
a time to weep, and a time to laugh;
a time to mourn, and a time to dance;
a time to scatter, and a time to gather;
a time to embrace, and a time to refrain;
a time to search, and a time to lose;
a time to be silent, and a time to speak;
a time to love, and a time to hate;
a time of war, and a time of peace.

Daddy
God has made
everything beautiful in its time.

Mojitola *speaks/reads the last stanza below solo.*

Mojitola
Whatever is has already been,
and what will be has been before,
and the past, will be called
to account.'[10]

Mojitola *closes the book. Scene transition. Music link 'Home Is where the Hatred is' by Esther Phillips mixed into the theme tune of a 1970s British TV show, e.g.* The Magic Roundabout.

Scene Four: The Foster Home

Quick slight scenic and small costume change to the foster home. Money is exchanged between **Daddy** *and* **Mummy Angie***, who are both played by the actor*

---

[10] Drawn from the Old Testament, Book of Ecclesiastes, chapter 3.

playing **Corner Man**. **Mummy Angie** *is a short, overweight, white, cockney foster mother. Private fostering is her business. She is dynamic, direct, quick-witted, fast talking, has a great sense of fun and a good heart but . . .* **Referee** *may also be the children in the foster home who interpret the action.*

Mummy Angie   Welcome to 'Blackfriars'. We'll do *you*, medium rare! (*She howls with laughter, looks to* **Mojitola***, explaining.*) Black – fryers (**Mojitola** *looks confused.*) Oh forget it. Now, I'm Ang. You can call me Mummy Angie but you can't call me Mummy cos I can't be your mummy cos I'm not Black. Get it?

Mojitola (*trying to get her attention*) Mummy Angie . . .

Mummy Angie   That's right.

Mojitola   Mummy Angie, my mum was white . . .

Mummy Angie   No need to split – (*Beat as she picks up one of* **Mojitola***'s curls.*) hairs.

Mummy Angie *manhandles* **Mojitola***'s hair, trying to figure out how she will manage it, combing it, bunching, it etc. During which* **Mojitola** *continues her speech below.*

Mojitola   . . . she was white and she came from Denmark. I was born in the hospital on Denmark Hill but she actually came from the country for real. I don't know where she is and I'm not allowed to talk about her, please don't tell Daddy I did, but I remember she kissed me here (*Indicates her forehead.*) and she was definitely white like you, Mummy. (*Corrects herself.*) Mummy Angie . . . (**Mummy Angie** *finishes with* **Mojitola***'s hair. She leads* **Mojitola** *on a tour of the gym/home.*)

Mummy Angie   That's right. *Mummy Angie.* Now what do I call you? What do I call you . . . (*She thinks.*)

Mojitola   Mojito –

Mummy Angie (*cutting her off*)   – Susan. Now, this is where ya sleep, (*Punches the heavy bag.*) this is where ya eat, (*Spits into a slop bucket.*) and this is where ya play. (*Throws the pouf like a medicine ball which* **Mojitola** *struggles to catch.*)

And if you stick by the rules, kid, (*Pointing to a list of rules on the wall such as 'No spitting on the floor'.*) you and me will get along just fine. What's that? (**Mummy Angie** *points to* **Mojitola***'s face.*) Bottom lip. Now, these are your new foster brothers and sisters. (*To audience.*) I only take Blacks, their mums and dads don't give me jip, (*Points to* **Mojitola***'s lip again.*) bottom lip. And a piece of advice, keep your guard up. You might need these. (**Mummy Angie** *hands over a ball of boxer's bandages.*)

Mummy Angie *goes to an upright speed bag, which looks a bit like a person. She clips the bag after she says a name.* **Referee** *spells the African names in BSL then speaks the children's names directly to the audience:*

Mummy Angie   Johnny –

Referee   J-i-b-i-k-e. Jibike.

Mummy Angie   Jenny –

Referee   J-u-m-o-k-e. Jumoke.

Mummy Angie   Kevin.

Referee   Y-i-n-k-a. Yinka.

Mummy Angie   and . . . Margaret, Margaret! Who only ever comes if I call her Kemi. Get over here and say hello! (*To* **Referee** *who briefly plays* **Kemi**.) A smile wouldn't cost ya. (**Kemi** *grins sarcastically.*) Oooh, look at those beautiful teeth. (**Kemi** *scowls.* **Mummy Angie** *calls to her son upstairs.*) Jimmy! Make sure the little one settles in. It's Susan. I'm off down the Elephant with this lot. (*i.e. the other children.*) (*To* **Mojitola**.) Right, I'll be back in time for the Spaghetti Western at three and if you don't mind, por favor, I plan to place my plates of meat on that poof with a Peter Stuyvesant and a nice cuppa Rosie and I don't expect to hear a peep out of yous. *Comprehendo*? (**Mojitola** *is baffled.*) Wassamaddah? Didn't they teach you English? (*Then softer.*) Uncle Jim'll see you right.

Jimmy, *played by* **Corner Man**, *sits with* **Mojitola**. *They are alone.* **Jimmy** *is in his early twenties, unemployed, rough, understated, slow-speaking, unlike his mother. The two watch* Captain Pugwash, *a 1970s children's TV programme.* **Jimmy** *laughs at the rude references and repeats the phrases, e.g. Master Bates, Seaman Stains, etc.*

Jimmy   Ha, ha . . . (*He starts to sing the theme tune from the following advert.*) 'Everyone's a Fruit and Nut case'. . . I like a nice bit a chocolate. (*He stares at* **Mojitola** *who is still holding her bandages.*) Here, Uncle Jim'll fix it. (*He starts to slowly bandage her hands, watching her intently all the while.*) So, how long you gonna be with my old mum I wonder?

Mojitola   Until my daddy gets back from Africa.

Jimmy   Africa? Messy. Could be some time. (*He continues bandaging the hands in silence, slowly, watching.*) You got pretty little hands. Bet they feel soft too. (*He continues bandaging, watching. Time passes.*) Touch this. (*Indicates his penis.*) Come on. Let me feel how soft your hands are. Touch it. Come on, Susan. It won't bite. (*A moment of sexual abuse is symbolized.* **Mojitola** *starts to shake. She screams her speech, an invocation.*)

Mojitola   Daddy!

Daddy come back!

Save me!

Daaaaaaaaaaaaadddddddddyyyyyyyyyyyyyyy!

Mojitola *shakes uncontrollably until she freezes on the sound of a loud bell. A huge puff of smoke with pyrotechnic, lights go wild.* **Muhammad Ali** *suddenly appears, like a superhero, in all his youthful exuberance and charisma.* **Jimmy** *magically disappears . . .*

Scene Five: Muhammad Ali's Surprise Appearance

Ali   TIME-OUT!

Mojitola   Muhammad Ali?! What, what are you doing here?! I thought you was in Zaire!

Ali   My rumble in the jungle's over with a long time ago. I don't fight no more. I have Parkinson's disease.

Mojitola   I saw you arguing with him on the telly. Did he make you sick?

Ali   No, it has nothing to do with that old Yorkshire bro. Parkinson's means I shake, and over that I have no control. Some said I was traumatized in the boxing ring but that, unlike my title, is disputed. Sure the fight game didn't make it no better. But I'm done fightin'. I don't move too good or talk too good and I put on a little weight, but don't you dare feel sorry for me, I'm not bitter. And I'm still pretty. Pretty as a girl . . . (**Ali** *looks in the mirror. Then he takes a piece of rope, attached to the boxing ring ropes, and starts doing a rope trick, which finishes by the end of the line.*) I mostly do magic now, give away my money, try to be a good Muslim: defend women, look out for orphans, tend to those in trouble, care for the sick, how do you like my trick?

Mojitola   Wick-ed!

Ali   Now it's late, and time for all God's children to go to sleep.

Mojitola   Don't go! Everybody goes. (*Trying to amuse him into staying, quoting him.*) Last night I turned off the light switch and I was in bed before the light was out. (**Mojitola** *jumps into bed.*) I'm faaaast!

Ali   You baaaad! (*He goes to leave.* **Mojitola** *stops him with her words.*)

Mojitola   Ali, I get really scared. Sometimes I wake up in the night and I don't know where I am. And I don't know who I am. And it looks like there's a man in the corner of the room but I don't know if he's real or if he's there. Can you tell me a story to help me sleep please? Sometimes in nice times my daddy tells me stories . . . (**Daddy** *re-emerges as* **Griot**. *It is as if* **Mojitola** *is dreaming her father is an African storyteller.* **Daddy**'s *role is signified by an African hat and sash. African instrumental music, e.g. kora.*) . . . like about Moses, the little baby in the basket and the burning bush and the two mums and the man splitting their child in half and Samson cutting his hair and losing all his strength and the writing on the wall and the lion's den and locusts and plagues and Pharoahs and slaves and techni-coloured coats and dreams and parting the seas and the salt and the thou shalt not and the wife of Lot who turned to stone when she looked back at Sodom and Gomorrah with the men and the men and the women and the women laying down together with the angel and all stuff like that . . . But can you tell me a new one please?

Ali   Sure, we'll tell you a story – the greatest of all times!

Ali *hands over the storytelling to* **Daddy** *as the* **Griot** . . .

Scene Six: The Griot's Story

Corner Man *plays* **Daddy**, *the* **Griot** *narrating the story, in almost a dance.* **Referee** *also performs the story in BSL. They interact at points. Kora music. Magical feel.* **Mojitola** *is transfixed.*

Daddy Griot   Not so long ago, in a land not far from here,
in the segregated South
of America,
there lived a young Prince
who was made from fine Clay.
'Of dark loam moulded.'[11]
He came from the centre of the earth.
He was soft, deep, brown.
There was no shape
He could not make.
Cassius Marcellus Clay.
In his lifetime he was both the most hated
and the most loved person
in the whole wide world.

Louisville, Kentucky had never been so lucky.
When he was born, he was such a pretty baby,
that everybody thought he was a girl.
He grew up fast as a jab, fast as a rattlesnake's stab.
His mother would say
'his mind chased after the March wind,
blowing every which way'.[12]
And if you thought you could predict what he would do.
He would always turn around and surprise you.

His favourite game was to have his brother throw rocks
and his friends would watch as he would dodge
clean out of the way!
His teachers said, 'American football he should play'
But that was too rough for Cassius Clay,
'No, sir, you get hurt in that game!'
There was not a scar, not a blemish, not a mark on his face.
If only
for Emmett Till
You could say the same.
Daddy Clay would show Cassius pictures
of Emmett, a boy the same age.
Lynched for winking at a white woman

---

[11] The Koran, Sura 15.
[12] Odessa Clay quoted in Thomas Hauser, *Muhammad Ali: His Life and Times* (London: Pan Books, 1991), p. 16.

and saying 'bye, baby' as she left the grocer's store.
They shot him, beat him, gouged out his eyes
Put a chain round his neck and threw him into the river.
He looked like nothing human as he lay in that casket.

Daddy *and* **Mojitola** *take in gasp of breath.*

Daddy Griot   And from that moment on Clay would never forget
what kind of a place America was.

But Cassius had it as easy
as a Negro could in Kentucky
growing up Black in the South, in the 1950s.
He wasn't rich but he surely wasn't poor
On his birthday
He could have anything he asked for.
His bicycle was his most prized possession
But when one day his favourite toy was stolen
he cried and cried and the tears streamed from his eyes.
He went to a policeman and said, 'You better catch him
and when you do I'm gonna whip him!'
So the officer said, 'Well, you better do it right
Step into the boxing ring
And learn how to fight'.

'Keep your guard up' they would say –
he kept them low like Sugar Ray.
'Box!' they would yell –
he'd slide then glide the other way.
'Slug!' and they would mug –
He'd just clown so free and gaaaay!
'Get down!' they'd shout –
he'd be on his toes.
'Move forward, Clay!' –
he would lean backwards.
Floating like a butterfly,
Stinging like a bee,
So young, so handsome, so prettyyyy!
'Box?' No, he was a dancer.
'Duck?' No he was a dodger.
'Punch?' He was a jester.
Miss? They expected a mister.
He said,
'I don't have to get hit'.
He fought with his wits as well as his fists,[13]

---

[13] Ali in his book *Soul of a Butterfly: Reflections on Life's Journey*, with Hana Ali New York: (Bantam Press, 2005) p. 117.

addicted to risk but then *you'd* be in a fix,
for when he hit it was *your mind* he would mix,
an illusionist with a box of magic tricks,
he had the best eyes in the business.
And the best legs,
And arms,
And hands,
And chest . . .
He was all heart.

Olympian!
So much greater than the Cassius of old.
He beat the Russian and he beat the Pole.
And for the USA won a medal of gold.[14]
Then he was backed,
by ten white millionaires.
He was the greatest.
He didn't have a care.
He was going home
Number one,
a champion!

But, when in his home town,
he dared order a vanilla milk shake,
In a 'whites only' segregated restaurant,
he realized that nothing he could want
could ever compare with true freedom.
The waitress said,
'We don't serve Negroes'.
Clay said, 'Good, I don't eat 'em either!'
And his gold medal shone in his broad gleaming grin,
she called, 'Boy – don't come back here neither!'
Cassius didn't wink as left, he did not say 'baby, bye . . .'
He just left the joint with his gold medal round his neck
and his proud Black head held high.
Crossing over to the bridge,
he looked up to the sky,
made a fist with his hand,
broke the chain from his neck,
threw his medal in the river,
and breathed out a sigh . . .

Towards the end of the story, under **Corner Man**'s *text,* **Mojitola** *starts to sing a short Yoruba song. This is a kind of ritual, a song of loss and love, of the cycle of*

---

[14] Ibid., p. 35.

death and life, sung thinking of Emmett Till, thinking of the young Cassius Clay. This
short song phrase will be repeated three times in the play.

Mojitola

Olukuluku, olukuluku o
Oun ni akoko wa fun (there is a time for everything)
Igba bibi ati igba kiku (a time for giving birth and a time for dying)
Igba wiwa ri ati igba sisonu (a time for finding and a time for losing)[15]

Daddy Griot   So the Prince became a professional.

But he was not just a fighter,
he was a gladiator,
a *performer*
and the boxing ring was his theatre.
And his first acting teacher,
was a world champion wrestler
named,
Gooooooorgeouuuus Geooooooorge!

Scene Seven: Gorgeous George

Referee *and* **Mojitola** *are children, chanting, excitedly anticipating the wrestling on*
television. **Corner Man** *quickly exits to change into* **Gorgeous George** *the wrestler*
costume – it should be fun, wild. Visuals of 1970s-style English wrestling,
e.g. Giant Haystacks, Big Daddy and those two camp blond wrestlers?!

Mojitola and Referee   Easy! Easy! Easy!

Mummy Angie (*offstage*)   Johnny! Jenny! Kevin! Margaret!

Margaret! (*reluctantly*) . . . Kemi. Susan! It's started!

Referee and Mojitola   Yeah! Easy easy easy easy!

Gorgeous George *enters improvising with the audience, teasing and provoking them.*
He speaks in a rich Yorkshire accent.

Gorgeous George (*offstage*)   I'll rip that bum limb from limb! I'll rip that limb *bum*
from limb! Grrrrrr! I am the greatest! Grrrrrrrrr! (*Grabbing* **Ali***, there is a vigorous*
wrestling sequence at full stretch through the text below. **Referee** *referees!*)

Gorgeous George
Cassius Marcellus Clay,
my advice to you is this:
'Keep on bragging, keep on sassing,

---

[15] By Juwon Ogungbe (1999) inspired by the Old Testament, Book of Ecclesiastes.

and always be OUTRAGEOUS!'[16]
They'll buy you and sell you and buy you and sell you out.
Attack with the clout of classy Clay clap trap.
Be a mighty mouth' Marcellus –
give 'em the Gasseus Cassius gas.
Use your lip, give 'em a lash.
Be bold, be brash.
Feel it, force it, fake it, you'll be famous in a flash.
You'll make millions of dollars,
mountains of cash,
you'll be rich,
sell out,
SUBMIT!

Exits, quick change back into **Corner Man**.

Scene Eight: All Talks Tricks

Motivated by the speech, **Ali** *rises from the floor announcing . . .*

Ali   I shall be . . . a poet!

I shall be a . . . prophet!

For my next trick.

Magic-show music. **Referee** *becomes* **Ali***'s magician assistant. She gives* **Ali** *huge playing cards.* **Ali** *deals the cards, improvising with the audience.*

Ali   Now, madam, I want you to shuffle these cards and shuffle 'em good. (*Shuffling his feet.*) I shall poetically predict when my opponents shall fall, I'll name the round and the crowd will come in swarms! (*After the audience member has shuffled the cards,* **Ali** *deals them to other audience members, improvising.*)

Now, people, hold the cards up high over your heads so the people at the back can see but I can't. Can the people at the back see the numbers on the cards? Good. Now if I get it right I want you to cheer, if I get it wrong I want you to jeer. Let me hear you cheer . . . jeer . . . cheer, jeer, cheer . . . (**Ali** *guesses the numbers, secretly indicated by the stage manager in the lighting box. Depending on the card number,* **Ali** *uses the following corresponding lines.*)

If you jibe me again he'll go down in *ten.*
I'm so dandy and fine you'll be mine in *nine.*
You ain't that great he'll land in *eight.*
If you want to get to heaven I'll lick you in *seven.*

---

[16] Gorgeous George quoted in David Remnick, *King of the World: Muhammad Ali and the Rise of an American Hero* (London: Picador, 1998), p. 120.

They'll cry it's a fix, I'll whup ya in *six*.
If you talk jive you'll go in *five*.
Don't block the aisles, don't lock the door,
This bum's had it, you'll go home after *four*.
You'll be prayin on your knees, so I'll cut it to *three*,
if that don't do I'll get ya in *two*,
if you tries to get rough – *one* is enough![17]

Ali's *card trick concludes with applause. The next fast frantic section switches between* **Ali**, **Griot**, **Jimmy**, **Mummy Angie** *and* **Mojitola**, *in different spaces, at different points in time.*

Daddy Griot   Out of twenty-one fights,
seventy-seven of the Prince's predictions were precise.

Ali   'I am a scientist! I am a scholar!'[18]

Daddy Griot   The sports scribes hated him, the press just baited him –

Ali   'It's scientific evidence! You ignore it at your peril!'[19]

Mummy Angie (*calling and watching TV*)   For Christ sakes will you shut your cake hole!

Ali   I am the greatest. The best that's ever been born!

Jimmy (*in* **Mojitola**'s *bedroom*)   Can I touch you? . . . I just want to touch you.

Ali   I am the greatest. I'm in a world of my own.[20]

Jimmy   Let me touch you . . . I just want to touch you.

Ali   As pretty as a girl I'll be the champion of the world! The champion of the world –

Jimmy   – who's a pretty little girl?

Mummy Angie (*annoyed because she can't hear the TV*)   I don't Adam 'n' Eve it.

Mojitola   See me . . . Save me . . .

Mummy Angie   I don't friggin believe this!

Jimmy   It's only my thumb.

Mojitola   Come back, Daddy!

Jimmy   Come on, bitch, come on . . .

Mojitola   Where's my mummy?

Jimmy   A little taste, a little tongue.

---

[17] Multiple verbatim text by Ali from http://en.wikiquote.org/wiki/Muhammad_Ali
[18] Ibid.
[19] Ibid.
[20] Ibid.

Mojitola   Why did you leave me?!

Jimmy   A teeny touch won't hurt.

Mojitola   I need you, ALIIIIIIII! (**Mojitola** *shakes vigorously which summons* **Ali** *again.*)

Jimmy   You little Black cunt.

Ali/Mojitola   You can't touch me! Nobody can touch me![21]
Your hands can't catch what your eyes can't see!

Mummy Angie   I am trying to watch the telly!

Beat.

Ali   Where do you think I'd be next week if I didn't know how to shout and holler and make the public take notice? I'd be poor and I'd probably be down in my hometown, washing windows, and saying 'yassuh' and 'nawsuh' . . .

Mojitola   . . . and knowing my place.[22]

Mummy Angie (*directly to* **Mojitola**)   I don't know where you are getting all this *language* from. All this talky talky back chat. You are bein' extremely truculent.

Mojitola   Whatever that means if it's good I'm it.[23]

Mummy Angie (*lightly*)   You lot ain't supposed to give me jip. Bottom lip. Now come here and have a cuddle, sulky six-year-old Sue.

Mojitola (*hurt that* **Mummy Angie** *hasn't even remembered her age*)   I'm *seven.*

Jimmy (*sinister, slow and low, he sings*)   Happy birthday to you, squashed bananas and stew, I saw a little monkey, and I thought it was . . .

Mummy Angie   Jimmy! That'll do. (*To* **Mojitola**.) Maybe Daddy will send a *belated* card, you'll always be related, awwww . . .

Mojitola *is very upset, crying.* **Mummy Angie** *cuddles* **Mojitola** *with real affection.* **Mummy Angie** *gives her a present, she opens it – a teddy bear. She gives a weak smile as thank you.*

Mummy Angie   There you go.

Jimmy   I'll give you ya present later. (**Mojitola** *squirms.*)

Mummy Angie (*noticing the TV*)   Oooh, look, cartoooooons!

---

[21] Ali to a white woman who wanted to touch him in Tom Wolfe's 'The Marvellous Mouth' in *I'm a Little Special: A Muhammad Ali Reader*, Gerald Early (ed.) (London: Yellow Jersey Press, 1999), p. 21.
[22] Ali quoted in David Remnick, *King of the World*, p. 125.
[23] Ali to Howard Cassell in the three-part documentary series *Muhammad Ali: The Legend*, part two *Ali Rap*. Revolver Entertainment, ESPN Enterprises, London: 2007.

Scene Nine: Yacub and the Spaceship – A Cartoon

Cartoon music. **Mummy Angie** *watches the TV(s). The animation features a spaceship and a mad scientist. It plays during the following scene.* **Mojitola** *sits outside on the doorstep, holding her teddy bear, upset.* **Ali** *'joins' her.*

Ali (*hushed tones*)   Look up. (**Mojitola** *looks up.*) See that? It's the spaceship.

Mojitola   What spaceship?

Ali   One day about seven thousand years ago, a bad, mad, scientist with a big head named Dr Yacub disobeyed Allah and created the white race off the Black . . . The mad doctor made the whites superior, and pushed the Blacks down into slavery. That period is coming to an end now.

Mojitola   What's that got to do with the spaceship?

Ali   Well, a spaceship took off with twenty-six yellow families living on it, circling the globe. They called it the Mother Ship.

Mojitola   The Mother Ship.

Ali   Soon they will come down and wipe out the white race.

Mojitola (*looking back at* **Mummy Angie**)   What they waiting for?

Ali   Once a year, they come down on the North Pole, put down a big plastic hose, and scoop up enough oxygen and ice to last them a year.[24]

Mummy Angie *gets up, comes outside to* **Mojitola***, kisses her and says.*

Mummy Angie   It's *Crossroads*. Don't you wanna watch the box with Mummy Ang? What you sitting out here for?

Mojitola (*looking up at the 'spaceship'*)   Waiting.

Mummy Angie   Aaah, din dins won't be long. I made a special tea for your birthday. It's jerky chicken tikka tonight. (*Like the tune of the TV game show* Blankety Blank.) Tikka tonight. Mmmm . . .

Mummy Angie *leaves licking her lips.*

Ali   This knowledge was brought to me by the one they call the messenger, the honourable Elijah Muhammad and explained to me by my friend, Malcolm X. They lead a group called the Nation of Islam who taught Black people to love themselves, that we were God's people, and that white people were blond-haired blue-eyed devils . . .

Mojitola *looks back at* **Angie***. She doesn't seem so sure about this.*

Mojitola   Devils? . . .

---

[24] Ali in conversation – see Remnick, *King of the World,* p. 133.

Ali   See when I thought about all the bad things that the white man had done in America, killing the Indians and enslaving the Africans, and when I pictured Emmett Till lying in his casket, and how even though they caught the men who did it nothing happened to them, and when I thought about my own life, places I couldn't go, places I couldn't eat and how I won a gold medal for the US of A and still got treated like a nigger in a place that was supposed to be my home, it seemed to me the white man could be a devil cos he acted like a devil. I don't believe that now, I never really did. I don't believe in Yacub and the spaceship neither. But I was young, and I was hurt and I was angry, and I was thirsty for a story, for a knowledge of myself. Angelo used to say I sucked in ideas like an elephant sucks in water, and I trumpet it out like an elephant too.[25]

Mummy Angie (*singing/calling from the kitchen*)   Ruby Murray in a hurry! Come 'n' get it!

Mojitola   Angie-lo? (*She looks at 'Ali'.*)

Ali   Angelo Dundee. Angie. My friend. My trainer. My right-hand man. (*Beat.*) Yeah, a white man.

Corner Man *now plays* **Angelo Dundee**, *who speaks in a strong New York Italian accent, as if in an interview.* **Mojitola** *listens to him.*

Angelo Dundee   When Muhammad first converted I didn't know what a Muslim was. I thought it was a piece of cloth. But I respected Muhammad and Ali respected me.[26] We never got into all that colour, politics and religion. We worked hard and got the job done. And boy when we won! . . . (*He wanders off reminiscing.*)

Ali   Malcolm was the first in the Nation to discover the truth, that colour doesn't make a man a devil. It's what's in your heart that matters. Elijah punished him. I turned my back on him. I wish I could tell Malcolm how sorry I am, that he was right about so many things. He was ahead of his time. But Malcolm got shot, before I got the chance.

Mojitola   Shot? By a white man? (**Ali** *hangs his head.*) By a *Black* man? (**Ali** *nods.*)

Ali   Malcolm was a visionary. He was ahead of us all.

Daddy Griot *sings a refrain of the African song underneath the above speech. Celebrating Muhammad Ali, thinking of Malcolm X. Again, a mourning ritual.*

Daddy Griot

> *Olukuluku, olukuluku o*
> *Oun ni akoko wa fun* (there is a time for everything)
> *Igba bibi ati igba kiku* (a time for giving birth and a time for dying)
> *Igba wiwa ri ati igba sisonu* (a time for finding and a time for losing)[27]

---

[25] Paraphrased from various statements in *Muhammad Ali with Hana Yasmeen Ali, The Soul of a Butterfly* (Ali on pp. 59–61 and p. 85 and Angelo Dundee on p. 99) with Hana Ali and Hauser, *Muhammad Ali.*
[26] Dundee in Leon Gast's film *When We Were Kings.*
[27] By Juwon Ogungbe, inspired by the Old Testament, Book of Ecclesiastes.

A clip is projected of Malcolm X addressing Oxford University students where he delivers and deconstructs an excerpt from Hamlet's 'To be, or not to be' speech. **Mojitola** *watches, listening intently. The clip ends.*

Scene Ten: Sonny Liston – The Bear

Daddy Griot   At last
The Prince had talked himself into a chance
to fight
for the heavyweight championship of the world!
There was only one problem,
he had to beat
Sonny Liston.
The most blistering fighter
in history.
Nobody thought Clay could beat Liston,
with one eX-ception: Malcolm.

Corner Man *plays* **Malcolm X**, *speaking to* **Ali** *in confidence. Getting 'him' focused.* **Mojitola** *joins in on this.*

Malcolm X   This is the battle of the Crescent and the Cross.
You have Allah on your side
Have no thought of loss.
You are David

Mojitola   Keep your eyes –

Malcolm X   He is Goliath

Mojitola   On the prize.

Malcolm X   and you shall be the first
Muslim champion of the world.
Do you know what that means?

Small pause.

Mojitola   Believe.

Brief movement motif based on Islamic prayer action. **Daddy Griot** *continues, articulating the story in expressive movement.*

Daddy Griot   The Prince directed his prayers to the setting of Sonny Liston.
And to the new religion, he signed up with an X.
But, he had to keep the fact top secret.
The Nation of Islam were considered a sect.
A dangerous menace.
Public enemy number one!

He must have faith.
The fight game was a gamble.
The stakes were high
and the odds were against him.
The media rolled the dice,
The mafia backed mean fighting machine
Liston
was lethal –

Ali   a monster!

Daddy Griot   – could he be beaten?

Ali *is depressed.* **Mojitola** *is trying to shake it out of him.*

Mojitola   Come on, Muhammad, he's not a monster, he's a teddy bear. A big –

Ali   – ugly

Mojitola   – teddy bear. Our area is full of Teddy *Boys*, (**Corner Man** *and* **Referee** *act out all the figures mentioned.*) British Bull Dogs, National Front, Skinheads . . . Thatcher Thatcher, milk snatcher . . . all sorts of monsters. But they got no chance 'gainst the rude boys and the Rastas. Believe.

You can beat him. You can beat anyone. (**Mojitola** *gives* **Ali** *her teddy bear.*) Here. Practise. (**Ali** *starts to animate it.*)

Daddy Griot   Cassius re-wrote the script and cast Liston in the role of a bear. And Clay would bait him, Clay would taunt him, Clay would tease him and act so wildly that Sonny would think Cassius was a mad man, his biggest fear since prison. Making Liston forget all he knew about boxing. And when he motored his mighty mouth for the money, the mafia laid it all on Sonny.

Ali (*puppeteering the teddy bear*)   'You big ugly bear. You too ugly to run loose, you big ugly bear. You shouldn't be in the boxing ring, you should be in the circus ring! You so ugly, when you cry, the tears run down the back of your head. You so ugly, you have to sneak up on the mirror so it won't run off the wall.'[28] You too ugly to be the champ. The champ should be pretty like me![29] (*To the audience, there can be some improvisation here.*) Let me at him, I'm gonna fight him right now! (*To the audience.*) Hold me back, no really hold me back. (*An audience member holds* **Ali**.) Let me at him! Let me go!/Angelo how many tickets we sold? Let me go! (*To audience.*) Whatever you do don't let me go! Let me go!

Referee *rings the bell, but the rhythm continues and it sets up a calypso rhythm/or West African highlife rhythm. All three sing and dance with boxing-style choreography. They are childhood friends again. Visuals of the first Clay/Liston fight play on the televisions.*

---

[28] Ali paraphrased, quoted by Wolfe in 'The Marvelous Mouth' in *I'm a Little Special,* p.15. The date of the fight was actually 13 September but it has been changed for contemporary dramatic resonance.
[29] Ali in the BBC documentary *Reputations.*

Ali

> 'Clay comes out to meet Liston
> and Liston starts to retreat
> If Liston goes back any further
> he'll end up in a ringside seat;
> Clay swings with a left
> Clay swings with a right,
> Look at young Cassius
> Carry the fight.
> Liston keeps backin'
> but there's not enough room
> It's only a matter of time
> before Clay lowers the boom
> Now Clay lands with a right
> what a beautiful swing.
> And the punch raises the Bear
> clear out of the ring.
> Liston is still risin'
> And the ref wears a frown,
> For he can't start countin'
> till Sonny comes down.
> Now Liston disappears from view
> the crowd is getting frantic;
> Our radar stations have picked him up.
> He's somewhere over the Atlantic . . .
> Who would have thought
> When they came to fight
> That they'd witness the launch
> Of a human satellite
> Yes, the crowd did not dream
> When they lay down their money
> That they would see
> A total eclipse – of the Sonny!'[30]

Ali, **Corner Man** *and* **Referee** *as a* **Trainer** *celebrate wildly around the ring, just as* **Ali** *did when he beat Sonny Liston that first time.*

Ali   Bear witness! Bear witness! I am the greatest! I want justice! I don't have a mark on my face, I upset Sonny Liston, I just had my twenty-second birthday! I must be the greatest. In the fifth round I was blinded, his paws were laced with poison, my face was burning, burning but I whipped him. Burning but I whipped him! Didn't Beethoven compose the fifth deaf? Well, in the fifth round I was blind and he couldn't hurt me! See, not a mark on my face. I am the prettiest. I want justice. I'm the King of

---

[30] Ali in Hauser, *Muhammad Ali*, p. 62.

the world! I'm a baaaad man. Eat your words! Eat your words![31] (*Now* **Corner Man** *transforms into* **Mummy Angie** *repeating 'eat your words' into which flows into her speech below.*) I shook up the world, I shook up the world, I shook up . . . I shook . . . I shook . . . I sssshhhhh . . .

Mojitola *starts to shake vigorously until she is catatonic, frozen. We hear and see white noise on the TV screens.* **Mummy Angie** *gives* **Mojitola** *a plate of food with alphabet-shaped spaghetti on it. She tries to get her to eat, repeating 'eat your words' and continues to do so until* **Mojitola** *has finished her speech above.*

Mummy Angie   Eat your words. Eat your words. Eat your words . . .

Scene Eleven: Telling Secrets

Corner Man *switches between playing* **Mummy Angie** *and* **Jimmy** *as* **Mojitola** *is frozen.*

Mummy Angie   . . . Eat your words. Eat your words. Eat your words. Eat your words . . . Susan. Susan. (*To* **Jimmy**.) I can't shake her out of it, son. (*To* **Mojitola**.) Are you alright? (*To* **Jimmy**.) She's been like this for hours. I'm in a right two and eight. Do you think she's had a fit or something?

Jimmy   Ignore her, Mum, she's havin' you on.

Mummy Angie   Susan. Come on. Snap out of it. Here come on, eat up. You like spaghetti alphabets. I got 'em special.

Wanna bit of hot peppi sauce? That'll get your tongue wagging. Ha. Come on.

Jimmy   Attention seeker. She wants a shrink.

Mummy Angie   Maybe she's just a bit upset. Another year gone and no card from her dad again. (**Mummy Angie** *takes the plate away then notices the word 'Jimmy'.*) Look, Jimmy. Have a butchers. See her plate. She's spelt your name. Funny? . . .

Jimmy *is tense, trying to bring her out of the catatonia.*

Jimmy   Susan. Stop play acting! Stop it! I don't care if it's your birthday, no one thinks this is funny!

Mummy Angie   I know what, I'll get her dad on the dog 'n' bone. Want me to try phoning Daddy, dear?

Jimmy (*nervous and aggressive*)   NO! You can't do that. (*Explaining away his aggression.*) It will cost you a bleedin' fortune, Mum. SUSAN!

---

[31] See http://en.wikiquote.org/wiki/Muhammad_Ali

Jimmy *freezes as* **Mojitola/Ali** *sings the prayer 'Allah u akbar' very gently and calmly; it is almost a lullaby. The tune is a composition by Abdullah Ibrahim (formerly Dollar Brand).*

Mojitola/Ali

> *Allah u akbar* (God is great)
> *Allah u akbar* (God is great)
> *La illah lil Allah* (There is no God but God)
> *Allah u akbar* (God is great)

Mojitola *steps onto a podium (the bench). Now as* **Ali***, speaking very calmly, into a microphone, addressing the audience.* **Refereee** *stands behind* **Ali***, surveying the crowd, wearing dark glasses like Nation of Islam security, interpreting.*

Ali   I'm not a Christian anymore. Black Muslims is a press term. The name is Nation of Islam. That means peace. Islam is a religion and there are millions of people all over the world who believe in it, and I'm one of them. I ain't no Christian. I can't be, when I see all the coloured people fighting for integration get hit by stones and chewed by dogs, and they blow up a Negro church and don't find the killers. I don't want to be blown up. I don't want to be washed down sewers. I just want to be happy with my own kind. People brand us a hate group. They say we want to take over the country. They say we're communists. They say we're terrorists. That is not true. Followers of Allah are the sweetest people in the world. They don't carry knives. They don't tote weapons. They find a time to pray five times in a day. I'm a good boy. I never done anything wrong. I never been in jail. Never been in court. I don't join marches. I won't pay attention to all the white women who wink at me. I don't impose myself on people who don't want me. I like white people. I like my own people. My name was Clay. Clay means dirt. Dirt you can mould. Even a child will tell you that. Clay was my slave name. If a man's name is Chung you know he's Chinese, Weinberg you know he's Jewish, Morning Star is a Native American. But Clay? Who is Clay? My name is: Muhammad Ali. And now you know I am a Muslim. Muhammad means 'worthy of all praises' and Ali means 'most high'. I know where I'm going and I know the truth, and I don't have to be what you want me to be.

Mojitola   I'm free to be what I want.[32]

Mummy Angie   Git up them apples and pears and don't you DARE play tricks like that again else I'll belt ya one! And just you let the social try and tell me different! . . .

Mojitola *goes to her bedroom.* **Mummy Angie** *speaks to* **Jimmy***.*

Mummy Angie   She frightened the life out of me.

---

[32] Paraphrased from Muhammad Ali's speech quoted in Hauser, *Muhammad Ali*, pp. 82–3; the sentence 'they say we're terrorists' is added for twenty-first-century resonance.

Jimmy   Growing pains. (*Calling.*) You're a fruit and nut case!

Pause.

Mummy Angie (*concerned*)   Jimmy, do you think I should go up and check on her?

Jimmy   Don't worry, Mum. Tell you what, I'll go and sit with her for the night. You go off to bed. Jim'll fix it.

Mojitola *closes her eyes in her bedroom, clutches the teddy bear and counts whilst* **Jimmy** *comes up the 'stairs'.*

Mojitola   10, 9, 8, 7, 6, 5, 4, 3, 2, 1 – time-out.

Daddy Griot   While the rest of the world slept, Ali became America's most abused and most hated.

Ali   Time to pray.

Ali *washes in the Islamic way and then prays during a quick series of still visuals of the anti-Ali magazines and headlines, punctuated by the famous cover for* Life *magazine where Ali is covered in bloodied arrows.*

Scene Twelve: Magic Fights

A shift to daytime, bright.

Daddy Griot   Ali's first defence was the Liston re-match. Muhammad promised a surprise.

Ali   Next up, ladies and gentlemen, we have the Liston rematch. I present to you the magic punch. The punch I used to floor Sonny Liston in the first minute of the first round of the very first the defence of my crown. May I have a volunteer? Yes you, sir. (*A male audience member is selected.*) Thank you kindly. Now I want you to count to three. By the time you reach two I shall hit you with the punch that floored Sonny Liston. Count to three.

Audience Member   One, two – (**Ali** *does not move.*)

Ali   Wanna see it again?[33] (**Ali** *laughs. Short drum roll and cymbal crash sound.*)

Daddy Griot   Many people thought Liston had been bought.
Had the mafia paid him to take a dive?
All we know is Cassius Clay was long gone and
Muhammad Ali survived.

Ali   I don't need crime to make a dime. (**Ali**, *like a magician, pulls out a coin from an audience member's ear.*)

---

[33] Ali in an interview with a sports journalist in the three-part documentary *Muhammad Ali: The Legend*, part two *Ali Rap.*

Daddy Griot   All he had to do was *perform.* And that's how the funky King from Kentucky made buckets of finger-lickin' money. The Nation of Islam were not amused, but Malcolm X didn't wear a frown.

Malcolm X   Though a clown never imitates a wise man, the wise man can imitate the clown.[34]

Ali   Now ladies and gentlemen, I present to you the next fool to try and challenge me in the ring. Yes you saw me beat the Bear, now it's time for the hare!

(**Ali** *takes a puppet rabbit out of a hat.*) The Rabbit, ladies and gentlemen, otherwise known as, Floyd Patterson! (*To the rabbit.*) 'You want to make some money don't you, Floyd? You want to make lots of money, don't you?'[35]

Daddy Griot   But the Rabbit didn't want to play,
he said 'I'll win the title back for America',
and refused to call Ali anything but Clay.

Mojitola   Clay! Clay! That's the name of a slave.

Ali   They must call me Muhammad Ali!

Into visuals of Ali's fights with Patterson and Terrell where he shouts 'What's my name?!' as he fights. Music could be 'I Don't Like Mondays' by the Boomtown Rats. An alarm clock bell sends us into the next scene.

Scene Thirteen: Shuffle to School

Alarm clock. Music fades out under the text. **Mummy Angie** *calls up to* **Mojitola** *who is now around ten years old.*

Mummy Angie   Susan!

Mojitola   I don't wanna go.

Mummy Angie *gives* **Mojitola** *a school bag with books.*

Mummy Angie   School.

Mojitola   I'm tired, I can't sleep at night.

Mummy Angie   Oh, Susan, not that old song.

Mojitola   They tease me, they don't treat me right.

Mummy Angie   Come on, shuffle along.

Mojitola (*impersonating* **Ali**)
'I've had appointments with danger

---

[34] Malcolm X quoted in George Plimpton 'Miami Notebook: Cassius Clay and Malcolm X' in *I'm a Little Special,* p. 33.
[35] Floyd Patterson in 'In Defense of Cassius Clay' by Floyd Patterson with Gay Talese in *I'm a Little Special,* p. 66.

Stayed fearless in the hour of horror
Chuckled in the face of catastrophe
Gambled with the odds of fate.'[36]

Mummy Angie   You're gonna be late.

Mojitola *walks to school. Music possibly 'Uptown Top Ranking' by Althea & Donna for transition.* **Corner Man** *plays a* **School Child** *who teases* **Mojitola** *with the text below.* **Referee** *is watching (signing) and stirring things up like a school child. They all move as if they are in a boxing ring.* **Mojitola** *dodges the taunts,* **Ali** *style.*

Mojitola   It's Mojitola.

School Child   Marjie Tiller.
Ma-Tallula?
Marjorie?

Madonna
Mogadishu
Magician
Mary Lee?

Mojitola   Call me Moj.

School Child   I'll call you Moji
Can I call you Molly?
We'll call you Mo
Call you Tola
Call you Mojo
Call you Smartie
Call you Jo

Mojitola   Mojitola

School Child   Messenger?
Methusa
Majestic
Margarine
Motley Moggy
Dodgy Podgy

Mojitola   Anything, except me!

School Child   Did I hear you?
Missy Tutu
Mossy Lulu
Moojie Two
Did your mummy and daddy hate you?
What the fuck did they do?

---

[36] Ali in the three-part documentary *Muhammad Ali: The Legend*, part two *Ali Rap*.

Is your daddy an African buju?
(*Fast.*) Did he cook a white girl in a pot to make you?
Mixed up with jollof rice and fufu?
Don't he like the taste of Danish pig stew?
Is that why he didn't want you?
Is that why they went and left you?
Did your daddy really hate you?
What the fuck did you do?

Imitating **Ali**, **Mojitola** *punches* **School Child**, *shouting after each punch.*
Simultaneous visuals of **Ali** *shouting the same at Ernie Terrell during a fight:*

Mojitola/Ali   WHAT'S MY NAME?! WHAT'S MY NAME?! WHAT'S MY NAME?!

Referee *becomes a teacher, stopping the fight by calling –*

Referee as a Teacher   Assembly!

Scene Fourteen: Assembly

They are all in assembly. **Mojitola** *sings proudly, visualizing Muhammad Ali's*
greatest fight, against Cleveland Williams, which is projected as they sing.

When a knight won his spurs in the stories of old
He was gentle and brave he was gallant and bold
With a shield on his arm and a lance in his hand
For God and for valour he rode through the land

No charger have I and no sword by my side
Yet still to adventure and battle I ride
Though back into story land giants have fled
And the knights are no more
And the dragons are dead

Let faith be my shield and let hope be my steed
'gainst the dragons of anger the ogres of greed
And let me set free with the sword of my youth
From the castle of darkness the power of truth[37]

The bell rings to signal the start of the first class.

Scene Fifteen: First Lesson

Mojitola *sits on a stool in school/boxing ring.* **Referee** *interprets as a school child.*
Corner Man *is* **Teacher One**.

Teacher One   Who has completed their homework? (**Mojitola** *puts her hands up.*)
Yes?

---

[37] 'When a Knight Won His Spurs' by Jan Struther, pseudonym of Joyce Maxtone Graham, in *Songs of Praise*
(Oxford: Oxford University Press, 1931).

Teacher One *stands behind* **Mojitola***, preparing her for a boxing match as she speaks the words below. He places gloves on her hands, a head guard on her head, and by the end of her speech, a gum shield in her mouth, thus shutting her up.*

Mojitola   Africa, Black, Cupid, Denmark, Energy, Freedom, Ghandi, Heat, Irie, Jimmy's Justice, Klu Klux Klan, Lesbian, Men . . . Nothing, Orgasm, Police, Queen, Riot, Socialism, Television, Unity, Vagina, War, X Malcolm, Yellow, Zion!

Teacher One   Wrong! You are all wrong.

On the last word, **Corner Man** *pushes* **Mojitola** *into the centre of the ring. Nina Simone's live version of 'Young, Gifted and Black' with piano plays; it sounds almost slowed down. A movement sequence ensues where* **Mojitola** *punches herself slowly, and reacts to the blows, under spotlight. The image should be quite disturbing. At the end,* **Referee** *rings the bell.* **Mojitola** *sits back on her stool, spitting her gum shield in defiance.*

Mojitola   It's a fix!

Teacher One   Detention!

Scene Sixteen: Examinations

Corner Man *and* **Referee** *immediately become US army Doctors/government officials. Music for transition, e.g. 'Another Brick in the Wall' by Pink Floyd. They remove the gloves, gum shield, etc., examine* **Ali***'s head, eyes, reflexes and mouth, poking him, pinching him, etc. unpleasantly. The actions are reminiscent of the capture of Saddam Hussein, a slave auction and a ringside doctor's tests.* **Corner Man** *as* **Doctor** *asks* **Ali** *various questions below, who tries to work out the answers.*

Doctor   Mr Clay –

Ali   Muhammad Ali.

Doctor   Mr Clay –

Ali   Muhammad Ali.

Doctor   Cassius Marcellus Clay, we are at war –

Ali *(interrupting)*   not in my name.

Doctor   I said *war.*

Ali   Not in my name.

Doctor   Boy, this ain't no time for games! War –

Ali   War. Huh. *(Like the song 'War' by Edwin Starr, 1969.)* What is it good for?

Doctor *(almost caught out, singing along)*   Absolutely noth – I ain't got time to play! Now, Clay,
answer the army questions to the best of your ability,
and you and I will get along just fine and dandy:

A   If military prisoners are detained in Cuba for seven years how many days in total will the prisoners be held without trial?

B   If Palestine is occupied from 1967 to the present day, how many years do the Palestinians live under occupation?

C   If 4,139 US soldiers are killed in a war in Asia in the first five years how many civillians are killed in total?

Ali   When I looked at a lot of them questions, I just didn't know the answers. I didn't even know how to start finding the answers.[38] I felt like one of my own enemies when I keep sticking him in the head, disturbing his thoughts, jumbling his pattern, mixing his mind. I stumbled and fumbled like a dyslexic in a book. Syllables jabbing, letters cutting, all I had given out felt like all that I took.

Doctor   Mr Clay. You are exempt from serving in the United States armed forces on the basis that your IQ is too low.

Ali   Hey! I said I was the greatest. Not the smartest.[39] I told 'em some good jokes though –

Mojitola   President Lincoln went on a three-day drinking binge, and you know what he said when he woke up? I freed whooooooo?[40] (*She belly laughs.*)

Daddy Griot   But if the truth be told, Ali felt ashamed. He could hardly read. Yet some knowledge only *he* could teach.

Transition to secondary school. Bell is rung.

Scene Seventeen: Secondary School

Mojitola *sings 'To Be a Pilgrim' in assembly, altering the last word.*

Mojitola

> He who would valiant be
> 'gainst all disaster
> Let him in constancy
> Follow the master
> There's no discouragement
> Shall make him once relent
> His first avowed intent
> To be a – [MUSLIM!][41]

---

[38] Ali quoted in Hauser, *Muhammad Ali*, p. 143.
[39] Ibid. p. 145
[40] Ali quoted in Mark Kram's 'Great Men Die Twice' in *I'm a Little Special*, p. 249.
[41] 'To Be a Pilgrim', John Bunyan, 1684.

Corner Man *and* **Referee** *play teachers.* **Corner Man** *is very like Margaret Thatcher.*

Teacher Two   Welcome to your first day at St Martin-in-the-Fields High School for Girls. 'Where there is discord, may we bring harmony. Where there is error, may we bring truth. Where there is doubt, may we bring faith. And where there is despair, may we bring hope.'[42] Now to your first lesson of the day – Geography. (*Unexpectedly called out of the class.*) Oh, there seems to be a problem, excuse me one moment, girls –

Corner Man *and* **Referee** *become* **Michelle** *and* **Donna***, bullies who take over the class. Engaging with the entire audience.*

Michelle   Right! Listen up, now I got your attention. I'm taking over dis Geography class ta ras. Fings are gonna change round here. It's gonna be Black people on dis side, and white people in dat side. Moji! What side are you on?!

Mojitola *looks shocked and confused. Sudden sound of fire alarm.* **Michelle** *and* **Donna** *sing/sign old school reggae style, celebrating the fire bell and sudden end of the lesson:*

Michelle

Fire! Fire!
Ding-a-ling-a-ling!
Fire bell a-ring!
Rice and peas a fight fe dumplin!

Mojitola *tries to sing and dance along with them, they leave her behind. She arrives at the mirror.*

Scene Eighteen: The Mirror

Mojitola *tries to imitate* **Michelle** *and* **Donna***. She tries to speak in a Jamaican accent, swear in patois. She gets it all wrong. She tries walking 'Black', flicking her hand, dancing, etc. She is no good at all. Tries kissing her teeth, she nearly chokes. The scene should be very funny.*

All these moves merge into shadow boxing, shuffling, i.e. **Ali** *practising his moves in front of a mirror.*

Ali   Kid, what *are* you doing?

Mojitola   Training.

Ali   For what?

Mojitola   How to be Black.

---

[42] Margaret Thatcher quoting St Francis, see http://www.margaretthatcher.org/speeches/displaydocument. asp?docid=104078.

Ali   Kid no one can ever disqualify you. You got nothing to prove (*Throws a few fast punches.*) and nothing to lose.

Ali *shuffles then punches the air fast. Possibly a burst of music – 'Am I Black Enough for Ya?' Bell.* **Mojitola** *shuffles to her next class.*

Scene Nineteen: The History of the Shuffle

Teacher Two   Today we will be having our mock English presentations. I hope you have all done your preparation. At O level we expect you to keep your heads down and your eyes up. You have three minutes each. So first into the ring we have Susan. Seconds out . . .

Mojitola   It's *Mojitola.*

(*Aside to the audience.*)

They can say metamorphosis and mythology,
metaphorical and mystery,
they can teach history, economics and war.
But that I am afraid
they cannot possibly pronounce.
That they simply
ignore.

(*To* **Teacher.**)

Mojitola.
It means I wake up to wealth, miss, or something like that.

Teacher Two   The clock is ticking.

Mojitola   The History of the Shuffle.

Teacher *disapproves.* **Mojitola** *presents whilst a collage of visuals on 'the shuffle' movement in the African diaspora is projected underscored by music, e.g 'Latin Shuffle' by Medeski, Martin and Wood.* **Corner Man** *and* **Referee** *to groove, shuffling . . .*

Mojitola   Shuffle –
To move with a scraping or dragging motion.
To rearrange, intermingle, confuse.
To equivocate.
Prevaricate.
Jumble, mix and shift.
To derange, disorder, disrupt.
A quick sliding move of the feet in dance.
An advance,
a retreat,
or both together.

Corner Man   One minute!

Mojitola *uses the whole classroom, demonstrating her message in movement.*

Mojitola   Shuffle has always been a feature of dances on the African continent:
Africans shuffled for celebration,
and shuffled in grief.
To maintain traditions,
and shuffled in chains.
Shuffled shackled in pain.
On the slave ships.
On the auction blocks.
Titilating their masters
who imitated their chattel
who imitated the white men,
choreographing their battle
on the stage.
Catholics especially liked to watch the Africans jig.
But Protestants said to cross your legs and lift your feet
from the ground
was dance and that was sin.
So the uncrossed and un-elevated shuffle survived –
as dance in disguise.

Corner Man   Two.

Mojitola   The ring shuffle was the most sacred space of all.
Round and round
circling the ring
shuffling their feet
and shouting to God,
pouring out their hearts
like a million Muslims in hajj.

And from the shuffle
came tap
and from tap
came jazz
and jazz equals
everything we are
and all we can be.
All our Black possibilities.
Our roots
and our routes
to being free.

So shuffle is a movement
is a memory
is a state of mind.

And when Muhammad Ali did *his* shuffle in the ring
he was doing so much more than boxing or dancing,
he was saying
Me, We.

Corner Man   Thirty seconds.

Mojitola   In 1968 the Black students took over Howard University singing:

I'm gonna lay down my shuffling shoes
We all knew what they meant.
I ain't gonna shuffle no more.
But guess what they were doing with their feet?

Teacher Two (*indicating* **Mojitola** *is in big trouble. Pointing the way out*)   See me.

Referee *displays a sign, dancing, as in boxing matches, end of Round One.*

Interval. Music.

Round Two

Referee *displays 'Round Two', dancing. Interval music fades out.*

Scene Twenty: Waiting for the Bus or Taking the Cadillac

Music, e.g. 'A Town Called Malice' by The Jam. At the bus stop/speed. Sounds of a London street. **Corner Man** *and* **Referee** *are* **Donna** *and* **Michelle**, *respectively, also waiting at the bus stop. They look at* **Mojitola**, *sneering and giggling.*

Donna   She's the one from the kids' home with a white mum and a funny name. She's looks like a –

They whisper 'lesbian' and laugh. **Ali** *'appears' to* **Mojitola** *in a gorgeous big pink Cadillac, the bench, with the bucket for a steering wheel.*

Mojitola   Wooooow, Muhammad, is this your car? It looks like an ice cream. I bet you get loads a girls in this don't ya? Can I have a ride?

Ali   Sure, kid, hop in. We don't have to sit at the back of the bus no more.

They drive. **Corner Man** *plays various passers-by and passengers. Sounds of a London bus mixed into African-American music, e.g. 'What's Goin' On' by Marvin Gaye.*

Passer-By One   Hi Champ!

Ali   Hi, baby, what's shaking?

Passer-By Two   Hi, Muhammad. Who's number one?

Ali   Are you blind, chum?

Passer-By Three   What's the latest?

Ali   I'm still the greatest.

Passer-By Four   Hey, champ, how many rounds for Cooper?

Ali   If he tries to get rough – one's enough.

Passer-By Five   You're the greatest, baby!

Ali   Hey, Angelo, could I have whipped Jack Johnson in his time?

Angelo Dundee   Baby, you could have taken anybody in everybody's time.

Rahman (**Ali**'s *brother*)   And that's the beautiful truth, brother.

Ali   *Salaaaaaaaaaaaaaaam aleikum.*

Passer-By Six   *Waleikum salaam!*

They pull up at a school playground near **Ali**'s *house. Sounds of a playground.*

Ali   Now, come here, all you beautiful Black children. (**Referee** *and* **Corner Man** *now play children laughing and fighting.* **Ali** *speaks to the audience.*) Only difference in me and the Pied Piper is he don't have no Cadillac. (*To the fight children.*) Stop that, catch you at it again and I'm gon bop your heads together. You don't fight your brother, even in play, don't do as I do, do as I say. I can't read, got a family to feed and I *need* to get paid. Now come on inside and I'll let you see some movies of me beatin' up the 'Bear' and the 'Rabbit'.

Mojitola *as* **Ali** *is now in his living room, threading the projector and talking to the children at the same time. We see the visuals of the fights he is commentating.*

Ali   Now, I'm gonna show the second Liston fight first, 'cause it last just long enough to warm up the machine . . . Here we go! Look children! Looks like a turtle chasin' a jackrabbit! (*Another piece of cinefilm cuts in. Ali vs Floyd Patterson.* **Mojitola** *scoffs at him.*)

And there *is* the Rabbit. Listen at 'em cheer. He's their great Black White Hope. Poor sucker! Now here I come! Boooo! Boooo! Boooo! Listen at 'em give it to me![43]

The booing continues in sound effect. It becomes taunts and jeering, bullying. **Mojitola** *is suddenly momentarily back at the bus stop.*

Donna and Michelle   Red skin reject! Red skin lesbian!

Back at **Ali**'*s house.*

Ali   That Rabbit went down seven times.

The phone rings as the fight plays out on the screen and stares. Possibly the intro of 'Hanging on the Telephone' by Blondie.

Scene Twenty-One: The Phone Call

Ali *hears the phone ring, picks up, speaks to a journalist who is giving him news about being called to fight in Vietnam. Simultaneously,* **Mojitola** *is now back in the foster home. She is also on the phone, trying to get through to her dad in Nigeria on a crackly line. Three worlds come together in this scene.* **Mojitola**'*s world, the* **Reporter**'*s and* **Ali**'*s.*

Ali   Ali . . .

Mojitola   Hello, Daddy? (*Pause.*) Daddy?

Ali   Don't call me that.

Reporter   Mr Ali.

---

[43] This section is mainly pieced together from dialogues involving Ali on pages 55 and 56 in Gordon Parks' article 'The Redemption of the Champion' in *I'm a Little Special*, p. 5.

Mojitola   Is it you?

Ali   Yes.

Mojitola   I want him not you.

Ali   Who are you?

Reporter   *Sports Illustrated.*

Mojitola   I need to talk to him. They might suspend me. And it's my birthday.

Reporter   How do you feel?

Mojitola   I really need to talk to my dad.

Ali   About what?

Reporter   About being re-classified for the army?

Mojitola   I'm going fucking mad here.

Ali   What did you say?

Mojitola   You're not listening.

Reporter   A boxer on the battlefield.

Mojitola   Where is he?!

Ali   Fight-in the war, me?

Mojitola   Please! Tell me.

Reporter   They have lowered the level.

Mojitola   I don't wanna stay here.

Reporter   So are you saying you won't serve?

Mojitola   No. They're nasty to me.

Ali   How can they do this?

Reporter   It appears it was just for you.

Mojitola   At home, in school . . .

Ali   They said I was dumb. Why do they want me now?

Mojitola   Why you asking me? I don't know –

Ali   Because I am a Muslim! Because they're scared of me. Because I speak up for my people and they wanna stop me. Because it's the only way they can draw blood!

Reporter   Will you accept the draft?

Ali   No way!

Mojitola   This is a waste of time.

Reporter   Any further comment?

Mojitola   Just give him this message –

Reporter   This conversation's over.

Mojitola   Don't hang up!

Ali (*to one of his workers off the phone*)   Get my lawyer on the line.

Mojitola   Tell him to come back and get me! Come back –

Ali   – now!

Ali *now speaks to his lawyer on the phone.* **Corner Man** *puts down the phone, and speaks into a mic, he is now a* **TV Reporter** *outside* **Ali**'s *house. Cameras flash.*

Ali   You heard the news? What the hell is going on?

TV Reporter   The most disgusting character to appear on the sports scene.

Ali   How can they re-classify me when they haven't seen if I'm better or worser or smarter or dumber?

TV Reporter   Join in the condemnation of this unpatriotic, loud-mouthed, bombastic individual.

Ali   For two years, they told everybody I was a nut, and made me and my parents ashamed.

TV Reporter   Should be held in contempt by every patriotic American.

Ali   I don't know nothing about the war.

TV Reporter   A sad apology for a man.

Ali   Yeah I know where Vietnam is, it's on the TV.

TV Reporter   All-time jerk of the boxing world.

Ali   Asia, man.

TV Reporter   A Black supremacist.

Ali   Man, I ain't got no quarrel with them Viet Cong.

TV Reporter   'Nothing but a yellow-bellied/nigger.'

Ali   *They* never called me –

All   nigger!'

TV Reporter   Self-centred spoiled brat of a child.[44]

---

[44] Ali paraphrased from Hauser, *Muhammad Ali*, pp. 144–5 and various newspaper reporters and writers quoted in Jack Olsen's *Cassius Clay: A Biography* (London: Pelham Books, 1967) p. 31.

Immediately back to the foster home. **Mummy Angie** *is fuming.* **Mojitola** *is now sixteen years old.*

Mummy Angie   Self-centred spoilt brat of a child! You heard the latest, Jimmy? It's her birthday right. So I give her record vouchers. She gives me a moody school report. Then she throws the present back in my face, says she didn't want vouchers for her birthday, she wanted *driving lessons*! She's having a bubble bath! (*To* **Mojitola**.) You're having a laugh. Where d'you get that idea? Ungrateful little madam. I ask ya . . .

Mojitola (*illustrating her argument in movement, elaborately around the space*)   I need to learn to drive so in two years' time I can buy myself a car, and move as far away as possible, from this pathetic place, and never have to get on the bus, ever again, with all the 'Donnas' and 'Michelles', who rant against apartheid race hate yet say 'yes, sir' and 'present' to names like 'Lyle' and 'Tate', and insult me with 'mongrel, red skin, half cast, half breed' yet they be listening on their Walkmans to Bob – I had a white dad – Marleeey, and they'll all be pregnant with ten million babies and no baby fathers, minding their Tyronnes, Charmaines and Dwaines and Junior-I-can't-remember-his-dad's-name, peck-pecking at their picknees and pick picking at their at their picky picky hair from losing all their minerals and using too much chemicals, cos by the time they finish their two stupid CSEs in textiles and home economies, I will already have ten O levels and four A levels, so I can drive away, waving 'bye bye', from my purple Lamborghini, whilst they're still smoking cigarettes and draw, sucking on bottles of Blue Nun, drinking Pink Lady through a straw, and dreaming – Big Dreams! (*Sarcastic.*) Of promotion: From stacking shelves at Tesco's on the Old Kent Road to checkout at Waitrose on West London's famous Ladbroke Grove. Dreaming from their balconies. Baby grows, bras and panties blowing in the breeze wafting the smell of shitty pissy nappies, as I speed. Away. And finally leave, the London Bo-*rough* of South-wark, (*now posh.*) crossing Kenn-i-ngton, St Ockwell, St Reatham, Batter-see-ah, Cl-aam and Bal-haam, heading to a green and pleasant idyllic country Un-I-versity. Actually.

Corner Man *shifts rapidly between playing* **Mummy Angie** *and the lower-toned* **Jimmy**. *The cues are picked up very tightly. Almost overlapping:*

Mummy Angie   OOOO – Uuuuuuniversity! You?! (*Shifts to impersonating a posh academic interviewing her.*) And what may I ask would you like to study and why?

Mojitola   Law or drama.

Mummy Angie   Ha!

Mojitola   Drama or law. I wanna be a barrister or an actor.

Jimmy (*understated*)   Nice. A paid liar.

Mojitola   An actor or a barrister – 'cause I LIKE ARGUMENTS.

Jimmy   F'kin' cheek.

Mojitola   And I am gonna need a car. No one will take me seriously without one.

Jimmy   No one will take you seriously anyway.

Mummy Angie   Well, why don't you call Daddy and ask *him* to buy you driving lessons?

Jimmy   – and teach you some manners while he's at it –

Mummy Angie (*calling round the room and then picking up the phone*)   'Daddy?! . . . Daddy?! . . . Daddy?! . . .' (*Sarcastically.*) Oooh, no answer. How strange . . .

Jimmy   Cheeky little monkey.

Mojitola (*enraged*)   You only want me for the money anyway, poxy bit of money you get out of me and my *name*. If I wasn't here to look after you'd be nothing. If I wasn't here to have a go at you wouldn't even have a job. I come from a longlonglonglonglong line of educated people. My grand-dad was the very first Nigerian accountant . . .

Jimmy (*singing*)   One banana, two banana, three banana four . . .

Mojitola   And my dad is an accountant too, or he will be soon when he comes back from Africa and takes his exams.

Jimmy   Five banana, six banana, seven banana more.

Mojitola   . . . I can do anything. I can be anything. And without me and all us Black kids in care you'd be nothing. You didn't make us! We made you! I don't *come* from you! I don't *belong* to you! I don't even *look* like you. And thank God, cos for your information, read the poster, Black is Beautiful . . .

Jimmy   Who you trying to convince?

Mojitola (*ignoring him*)   Black is best!

Jimmy (*sarcastically nice*)   Thought you was half-Danish princess.

Mojitola   Africa is the birthplace of the human race. We built the pyramids. This ain't my *home*! This is a dirty little pre-fab meant to be knocked down after the Second World War! Dirty nasty smelly pissy little bungalow on a nasty shitty tiny little island (*Indicating her small finger provocatively at* **Jimmy**.) that everybody here wishes was AMERICA!

Jimmy   Now that's below the belt!

Mojitola   You'd know all about that wouldn't ya?!

Jimmy   Say that again?!

Mojitola   BELOW THE BELT!

Climax: **Jimmy** *punches* **Mojitola** *in the face. She is knocked out cold. Blackout. Angry 1970s punk track kicks in, e.g. 'Anarchy in the UK' by the Sex Pistols. Quick costume change for* **Mojitola***, simultaneously indicating her change from child to adult and* **Ali***'s transition from clowning athlete to anti-war activist.*

Scene Twenty-Two: The Law

Mojitola/Ali *and his* **Lawyer** (*a white liberal male*), *played by* **Corner Man**, *are walking toward the courtroom.*

Ali   Why should they ask me to put on a uniform and go ten thousand miles from home and drop bombs and bullets on brown people in Vietnam while so-called Negro people in Louisville are treated like dogs?[45] Answer me that.

Lawyer   It will be easy, Muhammad, easy, easy. You probably won't even have to fight. Just play the game –

Ali   I done told you, the war is against my religious beliefs. God won't let me go down for standing up.[46]

Lawyer   Do a few exhibition bouts. Shake a few hands. Then come home a hero like Joe Louis.

Ali (*impersonating Joe Louis, scathing*)   Private Uncle Tom reporting for duty.

Lawyer   Think of the press, look what it did for Elvis.

Ali *gives his lawyer a dirty look.*

Lawyer   Muhammad they could throw you in jail!

Mojitola   What's Elvis got to do with this?

Ali (*to* **Mojitola**)   Don't knock the jailhouse rock. Everybody knows that brother's got Black blood.

Mojitola (*impersonating Elvis*)
    My hands are shaky and my knees are weak
    I can't seem to stand on my own two feet
    Who do you thank when you have such luck?

Tell him, Ali! –

Ali (*spoken, sarcastically*)   I'm all shook up.

Lawyer   Think about all you've worked so hard for. Think about your future.

Mojitola   Ali, try this one – Clean out my cell and take my tail to jail, cos it's better to be in jail fed than to be in Vietnam dead.[47]

---

[45] Ali quoted in Remnick, *King of the World, Muhammad Ali*, p. 289.
[46] Ali quoted in the three-part documentary *Muhammad Ali: The Legend*, part two *Ali Rap*.
[47] Ibid.

Ali   Baaaaaaad!

Lawyer   No good, Muhammad, this will do no good. Think of the kids, the young people who look up to you, think of –

Ali   If I thought going to war would bring freedom and equality to twelve million of my people, they wouldn't have to draft me. I'd join tomorrow.[48] So I'll go to jail. We've been in jail for 400 years.[49]

Ali *and* **Mojitola** *punch fists. They all reach the courtroom, which is simultaneously a police station.* **Corner Man** *plays the police officer.* **Mojitola** *is now in her late teens.*

Police Officer   Yes, love?

Mojitola   I want to speak to a police officer. (**Police Officer** *gestures to* **Referee**.) No. I want to report this to you.

Police Officer (*to* **Referee**, *note-taking in sign language*)   Take this down.

Mojitola   This is nothing but the truth. It happened a long time ago. But I still dream about it, a lot, in the day. It plays . . . It makes me feel strange and a bit dirty, and angry. When I was less than five years old, my foster mother's grown-up son, Jimmy, sexually abused me. He made me touch him, when Angie went down the Elephant, Elephant and Castle shopping centre. He held it in his hand. I thought it was a trick with his thumb . . . It's like a tiny video that rewinds and plays again and again in my head. Everything else is blank. I don't remember anything else. Except maybe the dark circles on the carpet, the being afraid. Time I guess has erased the rest. Sometimes I shake and I freeze. It's like I'm on pause but everything else is still playing, moving forward. (*Becoming distressed.*) And I'm stuck in time. Frozen. I can't speak I can't move I can't *feel* I can't – it's like my body is a prison and I want to, I want to move, I want to be released, I want to scream, I want to be happy and I don't know how and I'm scared that I never will. (*A pause for calm.*) I know there's not enough evidence. I am doing A-level Law at the moment so . . . But I just wanted you to know. And I wanted to tell . . . you. Because it's a crime isn't it? You're not supposed to, to a child. (*Beat.*) And I'm gonna tell you something else. Cos I'm a witness, not a grass, and abuse is abuse: my dad used to hit my mum. Beat her up. Pound her like a punch bag. Or wrestle her. Slam her against the wall. Do you know how that sounds? Flesh on concrete block. Hearing her screams and me static, senseless, immobilized with shock. Yeah, body shots mostly, until the end. Cos left hooks, upper cuts, jabs – they show up. People ask questions. But I remember, a straight right to her face, because it's my first memory, the first time I froze. I was cuddled up next to her on the sofa watching the telly, then he came at her and it came through me. Smashing her glasses into her face. Blood running

---

[48] Ali quoted in Remnick *King of the World*, pp. 289–90.
[49] Ali in Hauser, *Muhammad Ali*, p. 167.

down her nose, dripping from her chin. It's criminal isn't it? Beyond reasonable doubt. I was two. She was maybe twenty-two. I froze, for hours. She got away in the end. I understand. She's safe, somewhere. But I wanted you to know. I wanted to tell you. I want you to write it down. (**Mojitola** *points to* **Police Officer** *speaking forcefully, he could be her dad or . . .*) It's a crime! There are *rules*. (**Mojitola** *goes to leave, then changes her mind.*) And one more thing: you're supposed to look after your kids, dads. You're not supposed to leave them. Forget them. Forget you had them. Not turn up when you're supposed to, on time. Forget birthdays, you bastards. You're not supposed to leave them, to grow up Black, in Britain, alone with no one to show . . . (*Small pause.*) There's ninety-nine names for God, in Islam. Not one of them *father*. How was I supposed to learn to be? When I can't even pronounce my own name.

Mojitola *turns away. Gavel sound.* **Referee** *is a* **Court Clerk**, **Corner Man** *is a* **Judge**.

Court Clerk   Clay! The case of Cassius Clay!

Ali   Muhammad Ali.

Court Clerk   All rise!

Mojitola   Stand up. Stand up for all of us.

Judge   Cassius Marcellus Clay, you are sentenced to the maximum five years in prison and a ten thousand dollar fine. Do you have anything to say?

Pause. **Ali** *looks to the audience.*

Ali   Judge me? I am America. I am the past you won't recognize.[50]

Corner Man *switches to* **Daddy Griot** *narrating.*

Daddy Griot   A sentence so severe was unheard of.
Rapists were allowed to fight, murderers were allowed to box.
But a Black Muslim man taking a stand against a war?
That crime the state would never forgive you for.
They took away his fighting licence.
his passport.
his title.
And so the King, without a country, lost his crown.

Music to transition. Something by Bob Marley, e.g. 'Get Up, Stand Up'.

Mojitola (*protesting in the court room*)   No justice, no peace! Ali, you've got to appeal.

---

[50] Ali quoted by Sidney Poitier in the three-part documentary *Muhammad Ali: The Legend*, part two *Ali Rap*. These comments were not actually directed at the judge but are placed here for dramatic effect.

Ali   For real.

Daddy Griot   With legal bills for his appeal piling high, he had to find a new way of making a dime – fast.

Ali   While I'm out on bail. Get me Harvard. Bring me Yale! For my next trick . . .

Daddy Griot   This dyslexic took idyllic trips
and gave US college students top tips.
Yes, from pugilist to pundit,
he was America's most wanted.

Ali   I must be nervous. Look, my hands *are* shaking. My knees *are* weak.

Mojitola   You can't lose it now. You're the champion of the world.
Get out there and say something proud.

Sound of applause at the end of a university lecture.

Scene Twenty-Three: All University

Corner Man *now as a US university* **Lecturer** *will facilitate a kind of
'question time' with* **Ali** *and the audience, who are given prompt cards with
questions on them.*

Lecturer   Thank you, Mr Ali, for that very provocative talk. (*Addressing the audience.*) Now some of you have questions for Muhammad Ali written down on cards. Who has the first question? Yes, ma'am, go ahead.

Audience One   What do you say to people who call you an extremist?

Ali   I say the massa-cree of the Mohawks and the Cherokees was extreme, brutalizing children in slavery was extreme, fighting a war in a land that don't want ya there is extreme. If being a Muslim man speaking his own mind in the land of the free makes me extreme, well maybe I am. Or maybe I'm just in pain.

Lecturer   Thank you. Question Two.

Audience Two   Why do you hate white people?

Ali   Who's got time to be going around hating white folks? I don't hate lions either – but I know they'll bite.[51]

Lecturer   Your trainer Angelo is white Italian, Bundini in your corner is Black and Jewish, your Doctor Ferdie is Cuban . . .

---

[51] Ali quoted in Parks 'The Redemption of the Champion' in *A Muhammad Ali Reader*.

Ali   Yeah, they're my adopted family. So I guess you answered your own question.

Lecturer   Question number Three.

Audience Three   Is the the Nation of Islam a hate organization?

Ali   Elijah isn't teaching hate when he tells us about the evil the white man has done any more than you're teaching hate when you tell about what Hitler did to the Jews. That's not hate that's history.[52]

Lecturer   Ali, you seem a little stuck in the past, what about the future? Would you say you are pessimistic about America's race relations?

Ali   America don't have no future! America's going to be destroyed! Allah's going to divinely chastise America! Violence, crimes,[53] floods, folks will be quaking, the earth will be shaking –

Lecturer   – so you don't think there could ever be a change?

Ali   Such as?

Lecturer   Well, we have seen a white man on the moon. How about a Black man in the White House? (*Fragment of the Barack Obama victory speech over Jimi Hendrix version of the US anthem.*)[54]

Daddy Griot   But no matter what Ali thought of America, and what America thought of him, in countries all over the world they only felt love for the King: The Italians proclaimed – (**Mojitola** *rapidly impersonates the leaders described, with small costume and or prop for each.*)

Mojitola   'We'll re-build you the Colosseum!'

Daddy Griot   Gaddafi:

Mojitola   'Live in Libya, we'll start a Muslim revolution!'

Daddy Griot   Marcos joked:

Mojitola   'If you were Filipino, I'd have to have you shot.'

Daddy Griot   Nasser offered him his daughter:

Mojitola   'She's the best one I've got!'

Daddy Griot   Brezhnev invited him for dinner:

Mojitola   'You're the Black Henry Kissinger.'

---

[52] Ali in Hauser, *Muhammad Ali*, p. 121.
[53] Ali quoted in 'Playboy' interview in *A Muhammad Ali Reader: I'm a Little Special*, p. 141.
[54] The first performances of *Muhammad Ali and Me* were very shortly after the election of President Barack Obama.

Daddy Griot   And in the future . . .
Ali would meet Saddam Hussein and free American hostages,
would go to New York and save Jewish day centres,
and fool Fidel Castro with a fake rubber thumb . . .

Mojitola   Ali, Ali, Give us a poem?!

Daddy Griot   Even in America
the love for Ali outweighed the hate.
And when the Nation of Islam turned their back on him,
just as the young Clay had done to Malcolm,
Muhammad's own views outgrew his youth.
Then, after three and a half years of exile from the ring . . .

Mojitola   Ali! The Supreme Court overturned the decision,
you're free you don't have to go to prison,
you're free Ali! Give us poetry!

Daddy Griot   Muhammad Ali wrote the shortest poem, in history:

Ali   Me, we.

Mojitola   Meeeeeeeeee weeeeeeeeeeee! (*She dances around celebrating and ringing the bell with her packed bag, back to the foster home.*) I got my grades! I'm going to Uniiiiiiiii!

Mummy Angie   Well done, Susan. I am so proud of you. I know my Jimmy would be too. (*Looks to the sky.*) He will be looking down on you now and saying (*In Jimmy's voice.*) 'You're a clever little girl'. (*As* **Angie** *again.*) Gawd bless him. I miss him. They say the good die young. I just don't understand why, why was he running away from the police, why, on Blackfriars Bridge – (*Breaking, very upset.*)

Mojitola *smiles to the audience.*

Mojitola   'Better with cries and pleas
Or in the clutch of some disease
Wastin slowly by degrees'.

Mummy Angie (*not listening*)   – why on earth would he throw himself in the river? (*She breaks down. Although she is a comic character, her tragedy is very real. Takes out a handkerchief, blows her nose.*)

Mojitola   'Better than of heart attack
Or of some dose of drug I lack
Let *me* die by being Black'[55] – Muhammad Ali.

Mummy Angie (*composes herself*)   I know you haven't had it easy, Susan. But you've made the best of a bad lot and I respect that. You're on your own now, kid. Best of luck. Oh, almost forgot. I got you a leaving present. (*Handing an envelope.*)

---

[55] http://en.wikiquote.org/wiki/Muhammad_Ali

Mojitola (*underwhelmed*)   One driving lesson. Wow. Right, yeah, well, driving kinda represents like a masculinist capitalist anti-planetary hegemony and I'm not really down with that ideology right now . . . (*Returning the envelope.*)

Mummy Angie   Oh . . .

Mojitola   Thanks anyway, Ang. Maybe I'll visit in the summer.

Mojitola *exits,* **Mummy Angie** *waves her off with the handkerchief.*

Scene Twenty-Four: Smokin' Joe Frazier

Ali   But before that I am going to fight to regain my rightful title.

Daddy Griot   Against boxing's most bruising trail blazer, none other than smokin' Joe Frazier!

The bell-ring sets up the calypso/highlife rhythm from before, with new lyrics. All sing, sign and dance with boxing choreography. Visuals of Ali vs Frazier one.

Ali

> Ali comes out to meet Frazier,
> but Frazier starts to retreat;
> If Frazier goes back an inch farther,
> he'll wind up in a ringside seat;
> Ali swings with a left,
> Ali swings with a right,
> Look at Muhammad carry the fight.
> It might shock and amaze ya
> But Ali destroyed —[56]

Sound of a needle scratching off a record bringing the singing to a halt. Visuals of **Ali** *knocked down.* **Mojitola** *is knocked to the floor, reminiscent of* **Jimmy**'s *knock-out blow earlier.*

Scene Twenty-Five: To Fail

Daddy Griot   Joe Frazier floored
Muhammad Ali.
The old magic
was gone.

(*To* **Ali/Mojitola** *on the canvas.*) Good night, sweet Prince.

---

[56] Ali quoted in 'The Black Scholar Interviews Muhammad Ali' in *I'm a Little Special*, pp. 86–7.

This moves directly into **Mojitola** *in a drama acting class delivering a speech based on Shakespeare's* Hamlet: *below.* **Mojitola** *is very still, whereas* **Referee**'s *interpretation is very animated.*

Mojitola   To be,
To suffer
Slings,
Arrows,
Outrageous fortune,
The heart ache
The natural thousand shocks
That flesh –

Not to be,
To take arms
Against troubles
Opposing
And
Die?
Sleep;
No more;
To end
That flesh
Devoutly
To sleep;
Perchance to dream
What dreams?
What dreams?

When we have shuffled
We have shuffled
We have
Pause:
Respect
Calamity life.

Who would bear the whips and scorns
And scorns from time,
The oppressor's wrong
The proud man's
Pangs
Despised love
The law's delay,
The insolence of office
And the spurns
Takes merit makes unworthy

When he himself
He himself –

Who would bear?
To grunt and sweat under a weary life.
But that the dread,
The dread,
Of something after death.
The undiscovered country from bourn
No traveler returns,
Puzzles the will,
Ay there's the rub
Bear those ills –
Ay there's the rub.
Fly,
Fly to
We know not.
Conscience/cowards.
And thus:
Native resolution,

Pale thought cast,
Great moment
Name, action
And lose.
Lose.

Thin applause from **Corner Man** *who now plays the* **Acting Tutor** *with* **Andreas**, *a fellow student.*

Acting Tutor   That concludes our freshman exams. An actor is an instrument, so let's really get our 'Mojo' working with some feedback on the soliloquy . . . Yes, Andreas.

Andreas   Yah, sorry, Keith, I'm all for post-modernism but I've got to say, I've got a real problem with this.

Mojitola *kisses her teeth.*

Acting Tutor   Andreas, can you be more specific? Which aspect of Mojo's interpretation of Shakespeare's *Hamlet* did you find problematic? Was it her use of pentameter, relationship to scenography . . .?

Andreas   It's obvious isn't it? Do I really have to spell it out?

Mojitola   Look, I've never acted in my life before all right, how am I supposed to know? You said pick a play you relate to –

Acting Tutor   Mojo, just hold it there.

Mojitola   He's sad: his dad's gone, he can't talk to his mum, he wants his uncle dead, he fucks it up with his girlfriend –

Acting Tutor   MOJO!

Mojitola (*she mutters*)   Just call me Susan, all right, Keith.

Andreas   Am I the only one here who can't see it? (*He looks around, we can see people are nodding.*) Yah, you Hugh, do you see what I'm saying, Lotte, are you with me, yah? Harriet, Toby, uh-ha. You see, I'm not the only one.

Mojitola *speaks over the* **Acting Tutor**, *who continues, ignoring her.*

Acting Tutor   So you are refering to Mojo . . .

Mojitola   – Susan

Acting Tutor   being female and playing male . . .

Mojitola   – I wore a suit, what d'ya want?

Acting Tutor   playing in a working-class register . . .

Mojitola   – my dad was an accountant for your information

Acting Tutor   playing the Dane . . .

Mojitola   and my mum was from Denmark . . .

Acting Tutor   A prince, a classical –

Andreas   – No! Look, she's Black. It's, hello, *Hamlet.* You can't bugger the bard. A Black cannot play a white person. It's obvious, it's ridiculous, it's impossible!

Sound of sneering laughter as the students and tutor exit. Music for transition, e.g. 'The Ghetto' by Donny Hathaway.

Scene Twenty-Six: The Heart

Ali *and the* **Mojitola** *are sitting on a wall, having a 'heart to heart'.*

Mojitola *reads her grades on a piece of paper.*

Mojitola (*she screws up the paper*)   Prince of fucking Denmark – wanker! What's the point. I don't belong in their nice white theatre. I don't belong anywhere. I don't even know why I was born. If it wasn't for me my dad would have never married my mum, my mum have would never got beaten up, she would have never walked out, I would never have been left in care. All the shit, all the fuck-ups – it starts with me. And I don't know how I'll ever get past it all. I've got no one to talk to, no one who –

Ali   – you got me.

Mojitola   What are you talking about?! We're not even living in the same year let alone the same physical place!

Ali   You think reality only exists in time and space? You at college, you supposed to be smarter than that. Look, everybody feels bad, everybody fails, everybody loses. I lost to Joe and Joe lost to George and . . . presidents get assassinated, civil rights leaders get assassinated. News don't last long. The world moves on. There are more important things to worry about than some dumb-ass test.[57] At least we still pretty. Pretty as girls. (*Some girls pass by.* **Ali** *does a quick trick – presenting flowers to a female in the audience.*) Did I ever tell you 'bout the first time I got knocked out?

Mojitola   Got a feeling you're gonna.

Ali   The first time I kissed a female.

Mojitola   No! (*Laughing.*) Shame! For real?

Ali   Why would I lie? I fainted! Ten count straight out! I was so shy back then . . . How old are you now anyhow?

Mojitola   Eighteen.

Ali   Eighteen! You grown up as fast as a jab. Say, what do you want to be in your life?

Mojitola (*thinks*)   I want to be like you. Maybe I'll even play you. Fuck Hamlet. I'm gonna *pretend*.

Ali   As long as it's honest. Be a good girl. Live clean. Don't eat pork. Stay away from boys.

Mojiotla *indicates that she certainly will stay away from boys.* **Ali** *gives her an inquisitive look.*

Mojitola   I'll do my best.

Ali   Yeah, I have a feeling you will. (*Pause.*) Hey want me to explain my 'ladies trick'?

Mojitola   It's all right. I got a few of my own. (*She smiles.*)

Ali   You bad! I give up how I do all my tricks these days. It's un-Islamic to deceive people. The Magic Circle in England threw me out! But then so did three of my wives. We all make mistakes. Do things some people don't like. Sometimes people hate you cos they don't understand you, who you are, *what* you are. In God's eyes we are all equal. All that matters is what's in your heart. (*Making a fist and makes it pulse, like a heartbeat.*) There is nothin' greater than the human heart. What can compare to that? Now I can't read much, and you can imagine what's in my own heart when there's thousands listening to what I have to say. The Italians heard me and said they would rebuild the Colosseum so I could fight George Foreman there, but if that don't work, maybe I'll fight him outdoors right beside the pyramids,[58] or maybe in the heart of the jungle. Yeah, that would be something wouldn't it, a rumble in the jungle! . . .

---

[57] Paraphrased from Ali in Hauser, *Muhammad Ali*, p. 233.

[58] Ali paraphrased, quoted by Roger Kahn in 'Muhammad Ali: May His Tribe Increase' in *I'm a Little Special*, p. 133.

Afro-funk music to transition. Something by Fela Kuti, e.g. 'Fight to Finish' (live version.)

Scene Twenty-Seven: The Rumble in the Jungle

The music underscores. **Daddy Griot** *is dancing along whilst speaking.*

Daddy Griot   Seven years after America had robbed him of his rightful title, the Prince went to Africa in search of his lost crown. And when he landed in Zaire, they chanted, 'Ali, *bumaye*! Ali, *bumaye*!' Ali was amazed. There were Black people everywhere, chanting his name, Black people like him, running everything. A Black president, Black teachers, Black people on Black money. And for the first time in his life he felt at *home*.

Music fades out, into a series of political rallies, around the ring with the actors playing students, holding placards, chanting and clapping in rhythm. The chants are led by **Corner Man** *and underscored by* **Mojitola** *singing the version of the hymn 'Jerusalem' below.*

Student   This is what democracy looks like!
This is what democracy feels like!
We're here! We're queer! We're not going shopping!
Free the weed!
Meat is murder!
Free free Palestine!
Freee-e, Nelson Mandelaaaaaa –

Mojitola

aaaaaaand did those feet, from '79
Walk across England's mountains green?
And was the holy herb of God
In Brixton's burning market seen?
And did Ken's GLC collapse
Maggie, Maggie, Maggie out with your poll tax!
Three million unemployed! On yer bike!
Bombs and Greenham, riots and the miners' strike
The Falklands War!
How could we know it would be like this before?

Culminates in them all entering the ring and saluting the Union Jack flag above.

All   Ali, *bumaye*!

Ali   But before I go to work on George,
It's time to pray.

Mojitola *goes to a corner, her dressing room, sits on a stool, puts her head down and mumbles her lines, as if praying.*

Scene Twenty-Eight: The Dressing Room – 'I Am Going to Dance'

Corner Man, *as* **Stage Manager**, *brings* **Mojitola** *a dressing gown and puts it over her shoulders. She is now an adult, an actress preparing to perform, looking in the mirror.*

Stage Manager   Five minutes, Miss Adedayo.

Mojitola (*speaking* **Ali***'s words in RP, delivered minimally, talking to herself, psyching herself up to perform*)
See, I'm as pretty as a girl. There isn't a mark on me.
I am a great performer, I am a great artist.
The critics only make me work harder.[59]
George Foreman is going to meet his master.
I haven't had sex with my woman in two weeks.
And I am going to dance . . .

Now as **Ali** *calling to* **Corner Man**, *as* **George Foreman***'s trainer.*

Ali   Tell your man, he better get ready to dance.
We're going to dance.
Yes, we're going to da-ance!
You tell him to get ready.[60]

Foreman's Trainer   I'm not telling him nothing.

Ali   Tell him he better know how to dance.

Foreman's Trainer   He don't dance.

Ali   He don't what?

Foreman's Trainer   He don't dance.

Ali   George Foreman's man says George can't dance! George can't come to the da-ance! (*Beat.*) Tell him to hit me in the belly.

Corner Man *as* **Bundini** *takes* **Ali***'s robe off and psyches him up.*

Bundini   'You got to get the hard on, and then you got to keep it. You want to be careful not to lose the hard on, and cautious not to come.'[61]

Scene Twenty-Nine: The Rope-a-Dope

Music of 'Funky Drummer' by James Brown underscores. This scene is based on **Ali***'s 'rope-a-dope' boxing technique yet simultaneously suggests* **Mojitola** *having sex with*

---

[59] Ali in *Soul of a Butterfly: Reflection's on Life's Journey*, p. 73.
[60] Most of this dialogue quotes Ali in Norman Mailer's *The Fight* and the film *When We Were Kings* directed by Leon Gast.
[61] Bundini Brown in *When We Were Kings*.

a man who does not satisfy her. **Corner Man** *as* **George Foreman** *goes to the heavy bag and starts to hit it extremely hard, as Foreman did to* **Ali**. **Mojitola** *holds the bag.* **Foreman** *grunts. Her voice reveals no pain and is provocative and sexual.*

Mojitola   Harder, George.
Nothing.
More, George.
Hurt me.
Aim.
Harder.
Nothing.

Is that all you got, George?
They told me you had something.
Harder, George.
George, I feel nothing.
I thought you were the champion.
Come on, show me something.
Hurt me, George.
Nothing.

During the above speech, **Referee***, playing a female lover, approaches* **Mojitola** *and they dance together whilst* **Foreman** *is still 'banging' away at the heavy bag. During the dance there are visuals of Ali's fight with Foreman, the 'rope-a-dope' in the Rumble in the Jungle.* **Corner Man** *returns to playing* **Bundini***, Ali's corner man, seeing Foreman begin to break.*

Bundini   Oh lawdy, he on Queer Street now! He on Queer Street now.[62]

Ali *wins. Wild applause sound.* **Mojitola** *takes her bow after her first professional performance. The performer's dialogue moves rapidly between playing* **Mojitola** *and* **Ali**, **Bundini** *and* **Mummy Angie**.

Mummy Angie (*very emotional, proud*)   Oh, Susan! I always knew you had it in ya. And I always said it would come out one day. I always knew you'd grow up to be a thespian! (*Pronounced like lesbian.*)

Ali   Yes! I am the three-time champion. I'm the only man to win it three times. I fooled him with my rope-a-dope. George boxed himself out! He boxed so hard he got tired. I said, George, this ain't no place to get tired. I am the greatest champion of all time![63]

Bundini   Of all time.

Ali   Of all time.

[62] Bundini Brown quoted in George Plimpton, *Shadow Box* (London: André Deutsch, 1978), p. 326.
[63] Ali in Leon Gast's film *When We Were Kings*.

Mojitola (*to* **Angie**, *excited after performing* **Ali** *in a play*)   Was I pretty?

Mummy Angie   You was pretty.

Mojitola   Say it, Angie! Say it!

Mummy Angie   You was pretty, you was pretty! You was the greatest.

Ali   Was I moving? Was I fighting? Was I sticking? Was I a master?'[64]

Celebrating **Ali**.

Mojitola   Impossibilities!

Bundini   Black possibilities!

Mojitola   Pacifist,

Bundini   Antagonist,

Mojitola   Butterflies

Bundini   and bees. Necesaaaaary . . .

Mojitola   By any means. Contrary,

Bundini   Revolutionaaary,

Mojitola   Sexyyyyyyy,

Bundini   Masochist.

Mojitola   Is there something I have missed?

Bundini   He's the smiling pugilist[65]

Ali   Eat your words!
Eat your words!
He shook up the world!
I shook up the world!
You shook up the world!

Corner Man *and* **Referee** *repeat the words in bold below:*

Ali   'When I beat Sonny Liston I shocked the world. When I joined the Muslims I shocked the world. When I beat George Foreman I shocked the world. I am from the House of Shock.'[66]

Mojitola *starts to shake until all but her left hand is frozen.*

---

[64] Ali quoted in Ishmael Reed's 'The Fourth Ali' in *I'm a Little Special*, p. 205.
[65] The words 'smiling pugilist' are from a poetry tribute to Ali by Marianne Moore.
[66] Ali in Hauser, *Muhammad Ali*, p. 359.

Mummy Angie   Susan. Susan! What's wrong? What's happened to you? You look like you seen a ghost.

Mojitola   There's a man.

Mummy Angie   Where?

Mojitola   There's a man.

Mummy Angie   Who?

Mojitola   I don't know. I don't know who he is. Or what he means.

Mummy Angie   Susan . . .

Mojitola   There're a man
who sits
in the corner of my life.
The corner man.

Mummy Angie *holds* **Mojitola**, *then steps away becoming* **Daddy Griot**.

Daddy Griot   Even after he regained his crown Ali kept on fighting. Comeback after comeback, the doctors told him to stop. Ali described it as . . .

Ali (*very affected by Parkinson's disease*)   Like being in the near room to death.

Daddy Griot   He was was hit with blows that would have brought down the walls of Jericho.[67]

Daddy Griot *removes his sash and hat, indicating his storytelling is now at an end. He walks away, sad.*

Scene Thirty: A New Fight

Mojitola *is now an actor in her dressing room at the television studio. She is jaded, somewhat bitter and arrogant. She opens up a fortieth birthday card. It plays a ridiculous tune. She puts it down. Looks in the mirror – not pleased. Her hand shakes, it reaches for a huge piece of birthday cake. She wolfs it down. She looks at herself again. Disgusted. Sucks in her cheeks. Gets on the scales. Weighs herself. Changes the dial. Weighs herself again. Speaks. Visuals of Ali taking punches to the head, gaining weight, becoming ill, his last most painful fights, e.g. Ali vs Leon Spinks or Larry Holmes.*

Mojitola   I've done something new for this fight.
I have wrestled with an alligator
Tussled with a whale
Handcuffed lightning

---

[67] Frazier quoted in Hauser, *Muhammad Ali*, p. 325. The word 'blows' is substituted for 'punches'.

Thrown thunder in jail!
Only last week I murdered a rock
Injured a stone
Hospitalized a brick
I'm so mean I make medicine sick (*Winks her eye and sticks out her tongue in a grotesque way, as* **Ali** *did.* **Corner Man** *as a* **TV Floor Manager** *enters in a hurry.*)

TV Floor Manager   Tola! Make-up are waiting.

Mojitola (*barks rudely*)   Give me time! (*He exits, irritated.*)
There's a man who sits
in the corner of my life,
The corner man.
Shouts instructions from the wings
but he don't step into the ring.

Wants me to guard my mouth,
Wants me to spit out what's foul,
And just when I need him most,
He throws in the towel.

(*To* **Referee** *as if she were her mother.*)

And where have you been?
Referee.
Didn't you see that?
Didn't you see me?
Where were you
When I needed you
To step in
To step in between
To make it even
To keep it clean
To keep count
To keep watch
To keep your eye on the clock
To look out for the bites, the head butts and the blood cuts
To break the clinch
Let me breathe
Make it stop
Put an end to the punishment
When the pain was too much
Instead of letting me
become a bone shaking
drunk from the punches
COMEBACK!
After COMEBACK!

And WHEN and HOW am I ever to RECOVER?
TIME?!

Pause.

Where were you when I needed you
To make sure
they were playing by the *rules*
Playing fair.
Where *were* you?
Did you just not care?
And you (*To the audience.*)
Did you all keep score?
Who won? Who lost?
Or do you want to see more? (*Eats more cake.*)

TV Floor Manager (*extremely irritated he marches in*)   Enough indulging don't
you think? You're a fucking cliché. Two words: Make. Up. (*He exits taking the
remains of the cake with him, then utters under his breath.*) Turns.

Mojitola *paints her face with bruise make-up, quoting* **Ali** *in her own voice at first.*

Mojitola   They don't look at us to have brains. We are just brutes that come to
entertain rich white people. Beat up on each other and break each other's noses, and
bleed, and show off like two little monkeys for the crowd, killing each other for the
crowd. And half the crowd is white. (*Now as* **Ali**.) We're just like two slaves in that
ring. The masters get two of us big old slaves and let us fight it out while they bet:
'My slave can whup your slave.' That's what I see when I see two Black people
fighting.[68]

Referee (*signed and spoken*)   Cut! Great. Final take. *Me and Muhammad Ali.*
Rolling. Action!

Pre-recorded video clip plays of **Mojitola** *to camera. She speaks* **Ali***'s words simply.*

Mojitola   But I'll tell you how I'd like to be remembered: as a Black man who won
the heavyweight title and who was humorous and who treated everyone right. As a
man who tried to unite his people through the faith of Islam . . . True Islam, the
religion of peace. And if that's all too much, then I guess I'd settle for being
remembered only as a great boxing champion . . . and a champion of his people. And
I wouldn't even mind if folks forgot how pretty I was.[69]

Pause.

Referee   That's a wrap!

---

[68] Quoted in Remnick, *King of the World*, p. 221.
[69] Mainly from Ali in *Playboy* interview quoted in *I'm a Little Special*, p. 162.

Referee *and* **Mojitola** *go offstage, celebrating the end of the shoot together, singing, 'Muhammad, Muhammad Ali, floats like a butterfly, stings like a bee' from 'Black Superman' by Johnny Wilkelin; continuing from offstage: 'It's been too hard living. But I'm afraid to die. Cos I don't know what's up there, beyond the sky. It's been a long, a long time coming but I know, a change gon come, oh yes it is . . .' from 'A Change is Gonna Come' by Sam Cooke. They are simultaneously carrying out a quick change where* **Mojitola** *puts on a hidden harness for the final* **Ali** *levitation trick, and removes bruise make-up.*

Scene Thirty-One: Return

Whilst **Mojitola** *and* **Referee** *are offstage,* **Daddy** *comes on slowly, like a ghost. He goes to the heavy bag. He carries out a movement motif with the heavy bag. Carrying it on his back. Hanging off it. Enters the ring.* **Mojitola***, popping back in to the 'studio'/ring, to pick up her jacket before going off to the after party; she does not notice* **Daddy** *until he speaks.*

Daddy   MO-JI-TO-LA.

Mojitola   Daddy?

Daddy   What are you doing?

Mojitola   Daddy?

Daddy   What is this place?

Mojitola (*she looks around the set*)   My home. (*Beat.*) Where have you been all this time?

Daddy   'I have seen all the things that are done under the sun; all of them are meaningless, a chasing after the March wind. What is twisted cannot be straightened; what is lacking cannot be counted.'

Mojitola   I said where have you been?

Daddy   'Again I looked and I saw all the evil that was taking place under heaven. I saw' –

Mojitola (*finishing the sentence*)   'I saw the tears of the oppressed and they have no comforter; power was on the side of their oppressors, and they have no comforter.'[70] Same scripture? Same script. Someone else's words. Where have you been, old man?

Daddy   What did you say? . . . Who are you?

Mojitola   'I can't say who I am, unless you agree I'm real.'[71]

---

[70] Daddy and Mojitola are quoting from Ecclesiastes.
[71] Amiri Baraka quoted by Gerald Early in Introduction to *I'm a Little Special*, p. xv.

Daddy   What did you say? (*Ashamed of her.*) I don't think I can take any more blows.

Mojitola *goes to leave, then stops and says.*

Mojitola   I said . . . I said . . . I know where I'm going and I know the truth, and I don't have to be what you want me to be. I'm free to be what I want.

Long pause.

Mojitola, Corner Man and Referee   Aaaaaaah . . . Rumble, woman, rumble!

Ali   Now you're talking. Time's up. We're done. See my trick. See me. Me. We.

Ali *levitates. Blackout.*

The End.

Learning Pack by Reginald Edmund

Being an artist is a form of activism.
I hope that through this guide into a deeper exploration of Muhammad Ali
and Me by Mojisola Adebayo that you become inspired to get into the ring and
fight for the changes you want to see in the world.
– REGINALD EDMUND

Contents

**Quotes from an exclusive interview with the playwright are featured
throughout the learning pack.**

Learning Pack Introduction by Reginald Edmund

Since first being introduced to the works of Mojisola Adebayo, I've spent a great deal of time thinking about this play, about what it means to be a playwright, and what a revolutionary act truly is in a time where there is so much performative activism. Artists like Mojisola stand out. Not just with her catalogue of work that is absolutely beautiful and remarkable, but also the fact that she is a fierce artist and activist.

As the Co-Founder of Black Lives Black Words International Project, I was introduced to Mojisola through Simeilia Hodge-Dallaway, who described her as 'a true genius'. I admit now that I didn't realize just how true that statement was at the time. Together with Simeilia we commissioned Mojisola for the creation of *The Interrogation of Sandra Bland*, a rare play that envisioned one hundred women of colour speaking and enacting the words of pivotal activist Sandra Bland (7 February 1987–13 July 2015) during her harassment, assault and eventual arrest and death by police in Prairie View, Texas. Witnessing this work let me know just what truly is possible on the stage, and the impact one can make as a playwright for a community. Since that time, I've grown to know her as not just an amazing and exhilarating writer, but also a friend. Her work challenges and revolutionizes both the stage and the audience that is in attendance. Stirring inside of them the ability to see the world just a little bit differently that they did before. I personally have a great love for *Muhammad Ali and Me*. I feel like this piece does so many things that I love. I love how it channels the griots of Africa, because Black culture has always utilized performance to make revolutionary stances. As the new father to infant twin girls, I love how it centres a young dual heritage girl, finding herself in a world that struggles to allow her to live her truth, and despite it all she finds her strength. I hope that works like this empower you to stand in truth. And I love how it pushes storytelling in bold new directions. Mojisola Adebayo in my opinion is exactly as Simeilia described her – a genius! She pulls in the work of activism, blurring that with the stage in a way that few can or would ever dare to.

I wrote the piece to be produced in 2008. It was written in a time of war, and rumours of war around Iraq. A wave of Islamophobia was very present and I wanted to focus on Ali because he was certainly the most famous Muslim who ever lived, with the exception of the Prophet Muhammad. But for most non-Muslims, Ali was more famous. That felt really important to look and listen to a Muslim man – to somebody who in his youth had been considered a public enemy because of his conversion to Islam, his refusal to fight in the Vietnam War and his questioning of war. The play asks audiences to pause and question Islamophobia and the idea of who is a terrorist, knowing that by 2008 Ali was considered a great American hero – a great world hero.
– MOJISOLA ADEBAYO

The Play

Muhammad Ali and Me is the coming-of-age story of a young dual heritage girl growing up in foster care in the 1970s. Her struggle parallels that of legendary boxer Muhammad Ali also coming of age as as an activist, a freedom fighter and a Muslim with whom she forms a magical friendship in order to overcome her battles.

Mojisola holds no punches as she combines spoken word, dance, boxing, African a capella singing, original footage of Ali's fights, animation, pyrotechnics, magic, audience participation and 1970s Black pop music.

Time

1970s–2020s

Setting

The play is set in London and performed inside a boxing ring.

Champions of Activism Challenge: Gain knowledge, so you can impart knowledge . . .

CHANGE AGENT

Ali travels to Zaire and feels like he is at home. What statement is the writer making in regards to what and where 'home' is? Why is that important for Mojitola to know?

Ali refuses to be drafted into the Vietnam War. Do you think he is right for refusing to join the war? Do you think military service should be mandatory?

What are the pros and cons of celebrities and influencers getting involved with social issues?

REBEL

The referee uses sign language throughout the play. What do you think is the importance of utilizing sign language? How does it open the piece to a bigger audience?

Ali has a hidden disability where he struggles to read. Why do you think it is important for the writer to include this in the play?

CITIZEN

In the play Muhammad Ali appears whenever Mojitola finds herself alone and feeling scared. Why do you think he appears in these moments.

Why does the writer use the set of a boxing ring to demonstrate growing up in the 1970s?

The writer referes to the preparation of the fight as a ritual. How is it a ritual? What rituals do you perform every day or on a regular basis?

REFORMER

The adults in the play are supposed to take care of Mojitola and fail her. How are some of the ways they do this?

Our names are a distinctive way to reflect our personal identity and to show respect for another person's ethnicity and culture. What do you believe are the negative impacts of having a person's name mispronounced, avoided or misnamed?

Themes

Muhammad Ali and Me is a semi-autobiographical story which explores identity, self-acceptance and belonging.

Ali formed his identity by living life on his own terms regardless of race and popular opinion. From the renouncing of his 'slave name' to revealing that he had converted to the Muslim faith, Ali fights hard to showcase the complexity of Black identity. Although he did not march in the streets or participate in sit-ins for Black rights, he did join a religious organization that preached Black empowerment. He argued against the idea of patriotic duties of going to war and mocked his opponents in rhyme.

Ali unabashedly fought to be who he wanted, no matter the cost. It is his rebellion that saves and inspires Mojitola; his words soon melds with hers as she forms her own sense of self. We see Mojitola also battle with owning her name shortly after she arrives at the foster home and Mummy Angie, rather than learn her name, changes it to Susan. We witness her being bullied because she is of mixed heritage.

We experience the themes of self-acceptance and eventual belonging through exploring Mojitola's sexuality as well as her duty to stay true to her religious beliefs. By Act One, Scene Twenty-Five she starts her journey towards ultimate self-acceptance when she joins in with the political chants and yells out 'we're here, we're queer, we're not going shopping', all while simulatiously witnessing Muhammad Ali finally feeling like he's found home when he travels to Zaire to box George Foreman.

In this powerful coming-of-age story we watch as both Mojitola and her hero Muhammad Ali grow, experience defeats and triumphs, and ultimately find the beauty that is within themselves. These themes are key tenets to creating an empowering personal revolution.

Practical Challenge: The weigh-in

In this challenge, we will be testing what you are made of. Do you have the memory of a heavyweight?

Divide into two groups and nominate a referee. Each group has ten seconds to answer each question.

The group with the most wins by the end of the quiz will be the winner and will have earned bragging rights until the next challenge.

Your time starts NOW!

Question 1

What type of music is playing at the beginning of the play?

- A) 1960s
- B) 1970s
- C) 1980s
- D) 1990s

Question 2

Muhammad Ali was?

- A) A musician
- B) A painter
- C) A boxer
- D) A politician

Question 3

Mojitola's father leaves to fight in the war taking place in:

- A) Nigeria
- B) Botswana
- C) Belgium
- D) Vietnam

Question 4

Mojitola is sent to a foster home – what is the name of it?

A) Loving Home

B) Ingram House

C) Blackfriars

D) Young Home

Question 5

Mummie Angie replaces Mojitola's name with:

A) Becky

B) Karen

C) Louise

D) Susan

Question 6

What is the name of the school that Mojitola attends?

A) St Francis Academy

B) St Martin-in-the-Fields High School for Girls

C) Mount Saint Moses

D) Xavier's School for Gifted Youngsters

Question 7

The names of the bullies at Mojitola's school are:

A) Thelma and Louise

B) Michelle and Donna

C) Venus and Serena

D) Rizzoli and Isle

Question 8

The shuffle that Muhammad Ali perfects in the boxing ring originated from:

A) Michael Jackson

B) Dance clubs

C) Slavery

D) The Bible

Question 9

One of Muhammad Ali's biggest boxing matches is against:

A) Reggie Noble

B) George Foreman

C) Michael Keaton

D) Travis Bickle

Question 10

Mojitola delivers a monologue from the Shakespeare play:

A) *Othello*

B) *Titus Andronicus*

C) *Hamlet*

D) *Long Day's Journey into Night*

Question 11

A griot is:

A) A storyteller

B) A judge

C) A breadmaker

D) A tailor

Question 12

For not going to the Vietnam War Muhammad Ali was sentenced to:

A) Community service

B) One year in jail

C) Three years in counselling

D) Five years in prison

Question 13

Mojitola's father quotes from what book in the Bible?

A) Genesis

B) Exodus

C) Leviticus

D) Ecclesiastes

Question 14

Mojitola desires to go study at:

A) University

B) Trade school

C) Business school

D) Study abroad

Question 15

One of these characters is not in the play:

A) Corner Man

B) Referee

C) Cut Man

D) Mojitola

Champions of Activism Challenge: Step out of your comfort zone and make it your own . . .

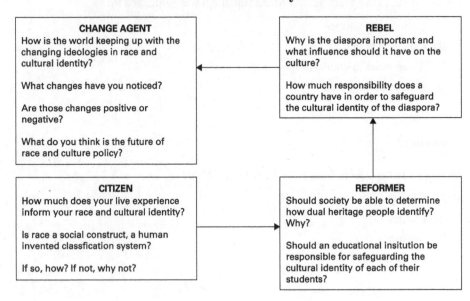

CHANGE AGENT

How is the world keeping up with the changing ideologies in race and cultural identity?

What changes have you noticed?

Are those changes positive or negative?

What do you think is the future of race and culture policy?

REBEL

Why is the diaspora important and what influence should it have on the culture?

How much responsibility does a country have in order to safeguard the cultural identity of the diaspora?

CITIZEN

How much does your live experience inform your race and cultural identity?

Is race a social construct, a human invented classfication system?

If so, how? If not, why not?

REFORMER

Should society be able to determine how dual heritage people identify? Why?

Should an educational insitution be responsible for safeguarding the cultural identity of each of their students?

For young people studying the play today, I would love young people to question when any group of people is pointed at and blamed for a social problem to always question that, to never take for granted that that's true. Whether it be discrimination against Chinese people being blamed for Covid or every Muslim being blamed for so-called terrorism, to just take a moment and pause and question what the media is telling us – make and find your own heroes and question everything!
– MOJISOLA ADEBAYO

Practical Challenge: 'The heavyweights'

Mojitola and Muhammad Ali have a weigh-in . . . Let's compare their characters and see how their narratives connect.

STATS	IN THIS CORNER	AND IN THIS CORNER
NAME:	**MOJITOLA**	**MUHAMMAD ALI**
LOCATION:	Born in London, England	Born in Louisville, Kentucky, USA
HERITAGE:	Black mixed heritage (half-Nigerian/half Danish)	African American
CLAIMING IDENTITY:	Is called a different name against her will by her foster carer but she reclaims her birth name	Changes name to reflect his joining the Nation of Islam and freeing himself from his 'slave name'
SELF-DISCOVERY:	Embraces her lesbian sexuality	Embraces the Islam Religion
ADVERSITY:	Fights to be accepted	Fights to be accepted
ACTIVISM:	Stands up against bullies in the classroom and her abuser at home	Stands up against the USA when they try to draft him into the war
POWER:	Finds power and freedom in telling her own story.	Finds freedom in performance

Which heavyweight will you challenge?

Can you think of someone that you consider a hero that is from a different generation or time than you? Why are they your hero? What are the differences and similarities between the world they grew up in and yours?

STATS	IN THIS CORNER	AND IN THIS CORNER
NAME:		
LOCATION:		
HERITAGE:		
CLAIMING IDENTITY:		
SELF DISCOVERY:		
ADVERSITY:		
ACTIVISM:		
POWER:		

Champions of Activism Challenge: Your agency is your superpower! How will you use it . . .?

CHANGE AGENT

What role does the media play in stigmatizing a group or people and associating them with social problems?

Can you identify examples in the past?

What can we do as an individual or a society to combat their influence?

REBEL

What can people do to diminish prejudice and discrimination against the LGBTQIA+ (Lesbian, Gay, Bisexual, Transgender, Queer, Intersex, Asexual) community?

CITIZEN

How can we shine a spotlight on social injustice?

What is the distinction between activism and radicalisation?

REFORMER

Institutional racism is a form of racism that is embedded in the laws and regulations of a society or organization.

Can you identify examples of such laws within schools, cities or countries?

What is the process of changing these laws?

What can you do to advocate for change?

Champions of Activism Challenge: Now, change the world for the better and create something new

CHANGE AGENT

Congratulations! You are a Change Agent!

Your challenge is to select a social issue you are passionate about. Create a list of provocations about this social issue and then develop an initiative for it. How can you get others involved? How can you support others?

We would love to see the results. Please send to info@beyondthecanon.com

We are certain that you will be a contestant inspiration for other with your words and actions. Nothing but greatness ahead!

Where Next?

Mojisola Adebayo published plays

Mojisola Adebayo: Plays One
A collection of plays published by Methuen Drama (2011)
Moj of the Antarctic: An African Odyssey
Muhammad Ali and Me
Desert Boy
Matt Henson, North Star

Mojisola Adebayo: Plays Two
A collection of plays published by Methuen Drama (2019)
I Stand Corrected
Asara and the Sea-Monstress
Oranges and Stones (previously *48 Minutes for Palestine*)
The Interrogation of Sandra Bland
STARS

Recommended plays that have a similar theme to *Muhammad Ali and Me* by playwrights from the global majority

Christina Anderson, *Good Goods*
Radha Blank, *Seed*
Lolita Chakrabarti, *Red Velvet*
Alice Childress, *Trouble in Mind*
Lydia Diamond, *The Bluest Eye*
Quiara Hudes, *Water by the Spoonful*
Antoinette Nwandu, *Passover*
Kemp Power, *One Night in Miami*
Caridad Svich, *Red Bike*
debbie tucker green, *Born Bad*

A Museum in Baghdad

Hannah Khalil

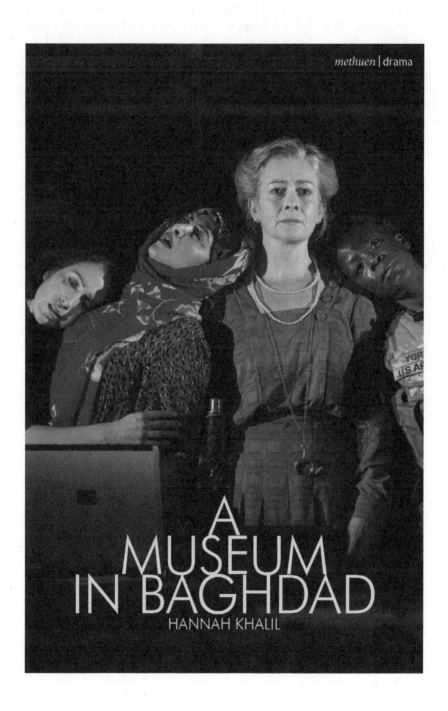

Playwright's introduction: Hannah Khalil

Sometimes you think a play is one thing – but later discover it's actually something else entirely. *A Museum in Baghdad* started life as a play about a woman called Gertrude Bell. It all started when *Plan D* was on in London and I went for a stroll around the National Portrait Gallery. There was an exhibition of Victorian Women Explorers, in which a picture of Gertrude caught my eye. The description card said something like 'aristocrat, explorer, diplomat, spy: travelled widely in the Middle East, spoke every dialect of Arabic and set up the Museum of Iraq in Baghdad'. I had never heard of Gertrude and set out to find out more – I read all her letters and diaries thanks to the University of Newcastle's online archive. Her life was so fascinating I decided I wanted to write about her. Then, not long after, the brilliant Arab British Centre in London hosted a talk by an inspiring Iraqi archaeologist, Dr Lamia Al-Gailani Werr. She was part of the team spearheading the 'clean up' job at the Iraq Museum in Baghdad after the American invasion and subsequent looting. Her talk presented images of artefacts stolen, destroyed, damaged and some returned. I was engrossed. Then at the end of the presentation her final slide was of a man in a blue boiler suit – the caretaker of the museum. She said, 'I always end my talks with a picture of him, because it feels as though he has always been there and as though he will always be there'. At that moment an idea crystallized in my head. My Gertrude Bell play wasn't about Gertrude: it was about the Museum in Baghdad and it needed to cover two times, the original opening by Gertrude in 1926 and the re-opening post-looting in 2006. These two times would be linked by a timeless caretaker who I would name Abu Zaman, in Arabic 'the father of time'. So began a huge rewriting and editing process that eventually became *A Museum in Baghdad*.

A Museum in Baghdad was co-commissioned by the Royal Lyceum Theatre and the Royal Shakespeare Company. It premiered in the Swan Theatre, Stratford-upon-Avon, on 11 October 2019. The cast was as follows:

Leonard Woolley	David Birrell
Layla	Houda Echouafni
Gertrude Bell	Emma Fielding
Kidnapper/Prime Minister	Ali Gadema
Ghalia	Rendah Heywood
Salim	Zed Josef
Nasiya	Nadi Kemp-Sayfi
Sam York	Debbie Korley
Mohammed	Riad Richie
Abu Zaman	Rasoul Saghir

Chorus performed by the Company

Miranda Curtis – Season Supporter, Swan Theatre Winter 2019

The RSC Acting Companies are generously supported by
The Gatsby Charitable Foundation and The Kovner Foundation

Creatives

Director	Erica Whyman
Designer	Tom Piper
Lighting Designer	Charles Balfour
Composer and Sound Designer	Oğuz Kaplangi
Movement Director	Tanushka Marah
Dramaturgs	David Greig
	Pippa Hill
Video Designer	Nina Dunn
Company Voice and Text Work	Kate Godfrey
Assistant Director	Yasmeen Ghrawi
Associate Sound Designer	Oliver Soames
Music Director	Phil James
Casting Director	Matthew Dewsbury
Development Dramaturg	Hanna Slättne
Production Manager	Carl Root
Costume Supervisor	Natasha Ward
Props Supervisor	Jessica Buckley
Company Manager	Pip Horobin
Stage Manager	Sarah Yelland
Deputy Stage Manager	Sharlene Harvard Young
Assistant Stage Manager	Adam Chesnutt
Producer	Claire Birch

Musicians

Voice/Percussion	Dunia Botic
Oud	Baha Yetkin
Qanun	Nilufar Habibian
Percussion	James Jones
Keyboards/Percussion	Phil James

This text may differ slightly from the play as performed.

Characters

Then (1926):
Gertrude Bell, *fifty-seven, from Durham, presently an archaeologist*
Salim, *twenty, Iraqi, Gertrude's assistant*
Professor Leonard Woolley, *forty-six, British archaeologist*

Now (2006):
Ghalia Hussein, *fifty-five, Iraqi archaeologist and director of the museum*
Mohammed Abdullah, *twenty-five, Iraqi curator*
Layla Hassan, *thirty-one, Iraqi archaeologist*
Private Sam York, *twenty-seven, American soldier (from the Deep South), female soldier*

Abu Zaman*, *a character who straddles time and space, trying to affect the future*
Nasiya, *an Arab woman who is timeless*

Notes

The set should be sparse apart from a large glass exhibition case. It is empty.

In addition, the space should begin sandless but gradually more and more sand is introduced throughout the play – emanating from pockets, things being moved, being swept in on people's feet.

Camera flashes can be just that or could be moments to reveal images from antiquity or the war that has raged outside.

At certain points denoted with * we have a choral effect using members of the company who speak in English and Arabic. This should have the effect of simultaneous translation like a signed performance, but with language and perhaps movement.

We are in the Museum of Iraq in Baghdad.

Abu Zaman *is on stage flipping a coin (ideally as the audience enter). When the moment comes he stops and says:*

Abu Zaman   It's time

People are conjured to the stage. We are Then (1926), Now (2006), Later (this could be in 50, 100 or 1,000 years in the future).

The space is filled with dignitaries and perhaps the odd soldier from Then, Now and Later.

There are three ribbons, three pairs of scissors, three important people.

Each important person cuts their ribbon.

Important People   I officially open this museum.

Abu Zaman* (*with chorus made up of* **Nasiya**, **Ghalia**, **Layla**)   Again.   مرة أخرى

Then

The space clears of people and **Professor Leonard Woolley** *and* **Gertrude Bell** *are left.*

Meanwhile **Ghalia** *and* **Layla** *are in a corner of the space with a laptop working.*

Abu Zaman *is fiddling with a coin – he knows he will need it soon.*

Woolley   You can't be happy here . . . Surely you'd prefer to be on site? Up to your elbows in dirt – I know you, Bell.

Gertrude   I'm perfectly happy, there's just a lot to do, but I've my system. Do you think I'll make it for the opening?

Woolley   You, woman, will achieve anything you set your mind to. But letting the king tell you when to open? I never thought I'd see the day . . .

Gertrude   It's not just him. The government too. You know that.

Woolley   You're not losing your touch are you, Gerty?

Gertrude   Careful or I may decide to come back to your dig at Kish . . . a bird told me there are some lovely artefacts being found, perfect for my 'little' museum.

Ghalia   Stupid idiot!

Abu Zaman   Another one?

Ghalia   Yes – cretins! If you are going to buy antiquities on eBay at least get an expert to verify it first!

Abu Zaman   How much?

Ghalia   This *h'mar* (*Looks for his name on screen.*), calls himself 'the appreciator', just paid a thousand dollars for a fake cylinder seal.

Abu Zaman   Do you follow the real ones or only the fakes?

Ghalia   I report the real ones – breaking the laws of antiquities. I laugh at the donkeys who buy the fakes!

Layla   I'm amazed you make the time. The basements are still in chaos – trying to get a list of everything stolen or damaged will take a lifetime.

Ghalia   These people need to be brought to justice. They can't just take what they want. This is our country and we have to protect it.

She returns to the screen.

Woolley   Has he been? The king – seen what you're doing . . . how much is left to do.

Gertrude   I expect him any day. But I'm not worried – if you agree to help me plan this place I'll surely make the opening in time.

Woolley   The question is – what's in it for me?

Gertrude   The Englishman's mantra. What do you want?

Woolley   Well, once you are open perhaps you'd consider loaning us a few items? Your goddess for example. (*Indicating empty glass cabinet.*)

Gertrude   I won't lend her unless I have it in writing that she'll return: I know your 'borrowing' and don't forget the Iraq laws of antiquities.

Woolley   How could I? You and your laws, like a little girl who changes the rules of the game to suit her.

Gertrude   What are you complaining about? Before my laws you could barely dig here.

Woolley   Yes but now *you* get the pick of the finds.

Gertrude   This isn't about me – it's about creating unity, nationhood.

Woolley   Isn't that why we've crowned a king?

Gertrude   It's about galvanizing an identity for the people of Iraq.

Woolley   Ha! There was no such country till five years ago –

Gertrude   That's exactly my point.

Woolley   From what I hear they don't think your laws are stringent enough.

Gertrude   Of course they are. What is found in their country belongs to them. But *you lot* do need an incentive to dig in the first place.

Woolley   I predict it'll all be back to the BM in time for tea when civil war erupts again and they go back to their tribes.

A beat.

Gertrude   What do you think, Abu Zaman – as an Iraqi?

Woolley   He's no fool – he knows she'd be safer in Blighty.

Abu Zaman* (*with chorus of* **Ghalia**)   Safer?   أكثر أماناً؟

Gertrude   Don't you be swayed by him. Come on let's do this the Arab way – *maktouba* – let's toss a coin for it.

Abu Zaman   Allow me.

He tosses a coin. In doing so he affects the timeline. You can indicate or mark this 'magical' moment in production or not as you see fit.

Gertrude *calls 'heads'.* **Abu Zaman** *shows them both the coin – tails.* **Woolley** *is ecstatic.*

Woolley   Tails! I win! She comes to England!

Gertrude   But my statue!

Woolley   Ah, ah! It's not yours – it belongs to the 'people of Iraq', remember?

Gertrude   Abu Zaman – how could you?

Woolley   Don't blame the poor chap, he can't control the toss of a coin –

Abu Zaman   She'll be safer in England – Professor Woolley said so.

Gertrude   If she survives the journey in one piece. She doesn't belong there.

Abu Zaman* (*with chorus of* **Ghalia**)   It's dangerous?   خطر؟

Woolley   Don't panic him! Come on, old boy – I'll give you the shipping details.

Gertrude   But the opening.

Woolley   You can keep her for that, Gertie – send her after. Why are you so upset?

Gertrude   I have high hopes for this place. I don't want you interfering – it could be a great museum.

Woolley   Don't be a bad loser.

Gertrude   First her – what next? It's a slippery slope . . .

Woolley   *You* could always chaperone her.

Abu Zaman   She *will* be safer in England won't she, Professor Woolley?

Woolley   Relax, old boy, we treat our treasures with nothing but respect.

He has gone.

Abu Zaman *places his coin on the floor and goes behind the glass to see what will happen.*

Gertrude *stands staring at the glass cabinet from one side.*

Ghalia *'s attention is also captured by it.*

We are simultaneously Then/Now/Later.

Abu Zaman *goes behind the glass cabinet and looks through it as though it is a crystal ball – a vision of what's to come.*

Through it he sees **Mohammed** *(Later). He is older. He is smoking a cigarette – on a break from his work at the museum. He wears a lanyard around his neck – it says he*

*is the director of the museum. He holds it and looks at it then spots the coin and bends
to get it. As he does so three masked men enter and approach him. They grab him, put
a pillow over his head and hustle him out of the space.*

Abu Zaman *bangs his hand on the glass, frustrated.*

A camera flashes.

Under the chorus detailed below we see the exact same action of **Mohammed**'s
kidnap once more played in a clean, matter-of-fact way.

Then/Now/Later

Abu Zaman* (*with chorus*)

What if –	ماذا لو
You could play a moment	بإمكانِكَ ان تُعيدَّ اللحَظة
Again	مرةً أُخرى

He tosses a coin.

And again	ومرةٌ أخرى

He tosses a coin.

And again	ومرةٌ أخرى

He tosses a coin.

Torture	تَعذيب
Unless	الا إذا
You could unpick the stitches	يُمكنُكَ ان تُزيلَ الغُرَز
Be ready to start again	وكُنتَ مُستَعِداً أن تَبدءَ من جَديد
Try again . . .	وان تُحاولَ مرةً أُخرى
Make it better . . .	وان تَجعلَ كُلَ شيءٍ أفضل
The past you can't change	لا أحَدَ يُمكِنُهُ تَغييرُ الماضي
But the future . . .	
we must all try to make the future the best it can be For who knows what's to come?	لكِنَّ المُستقبل . . . يَجِبُ علينا جميعاً ان نَجعَلهُ أفضَلَ ما يُمكِن فمن يَعرفُ ماذا سَيحدُث؟
Only a person who predicts the future.	
Fatahit Al Fahl – A fortune teller	سِوى الشَخصِّ الذي يَتَنَبأُ بالمُستَقبِل
What if it was this person's job – not with a looking glass or magic but with calculations.	وماذا لو كانت تلكَ مِهنَتُها..مُعتَمِدَةً لا على مِرآه ولا على تَعاويذَ سِحرية. وإنما على الحِسابات . . .

With knowledge. A microphone. A camera.

بالمعرفة.. بميكروفون.. بكاميرا..

A clear sight of what had happened in the distant past, as well as recent history, with an understanding of human nature – patterns of behaviour.

ورؤيةٍ واضِحَةٍ لِما حَدَثَ في الماضي البَعيد والتاريخ الحديث، وفَهمٍ لطَبيعةِ الإنسان – لأنماطِ سُلوك البَشَرْ . . .

In 5, 4, 3, 2, 1

٥،٤،٣،٢،١

And what if this person was asked routinely –
What do you think will happen next?

وماذا لو سُئِلَ هذا الشخص بصورَةٍ روتينية

مالذي سَيحدُثُ فيما بعد؟

And they had to offer up their thoughts – what would be the text?

وكان عَليهمْ طَرحَ أفكارِهِم.. مالذي سَيُحكى؟

A leader gone.

القائدُ سَقَط.

Showers of bombs

أمطارٌ من القذائف..

Playing cards rain down over the stage

Enemies uniting.

أعداءٌ يَتِّحِدّون..

People in hiding.

أناسٌ مُختَبِئون..

The wrong kind of aid.

مُساعداتٌ فاشِلة

Military heroes made.

أبطالٌ عَسكريون يُخلَقون..

Families fled.

عائلاتٌ هاربة

Children dead.

أطفالٌ مَيتون.

Seas

بحار..

Bodies

أجساد..

Perhaps.

رُبمَا . . .

All possible.

Of course.

كُلُّ شيءٍ مُمكن. بالتأكيد

But in the end. They won't dig down far enough

لكن ،وفي النهاية

لن يَتَعمَقوا بما فيه الكفاية

Can't imagine.

لم يكونوا قادرين على تَخيُّلِ

What's to come.

ما سيأتي

What will happen next . . .

ما الذي سَيحدُثُ فيما بعد..

Now

Layla *and* **Mohammed** *are working, logging items.*

Gertrude *writes in a corner.*

Private Sam York *collects the playing cards from the floor.*

York   Sure is hot.

A beat.

Like an oven.

Layla   Shame your colleagues didn't realize.

York   What?

Layla   That while they sat back and watched, the looters were taking pipes and wires as well as artefacts, making the building unpleasant for you now.

Pause.

York   The director sent me back here. She had to see the minister. Is there anything you want me to do?

Layla   A tank would have been nice. But it's a bit late now.

A beat.

York   I don't know much about the ins and outs of what happened here yet, I wasn't part of the initial force, but I do know one tank on its own wouldn't have been able to do much.

Layla   What are you talking about – a huge US tank on the grass outside would have the same effect as an ugly guard dog.

York   What most civilians don't realize is a stationary tank is like a death trap. They have blind spots like a car . . . you need at least two.

Mohammed (*to* **Layla**)   You've been schooled. By an American. Ouch!

Layla   Well, then, two would have been nice.

York   And infantry as well – and once you get infantry you get a big shoot-up and I can tell you for nothing this here museum'd be a big old pile of rubble if that had happened.

Mohammed   At least this historic building is still standing.

Layla *looks annoyed.*

Layla   Historic building!

York *has collected all the playing cards and lays them out on the floor for a game of patience.*

They continue their individual tasks in tense silence.

Pause.

York   Hey, awesome.

A beat.

Mohammed   I'll bite. What is so awesome?

York   I just saw this mask in the amnesty room, someone brought it back.

She shows him a picture on the back of one of her playing cards.

Mohammed   The mask of Warka.

York   She made it home.

Layla   One of the first representations of a human face . . . amazing she came back – there are some who would call her sacrilegious.

York   She looks perfect to me

Layla   Depictions of beings with souls are haram.

Mohammed   Forbidden – but only crazy zealots think that . . .

Layla   How do you know I'm not one of those?

Mohammed   I know. (*A beat.*) I heard they were giving you cards with sites and artefacts on – I never saw them – can I look?

York   Sure – let's play. You know rummy?

Mohammed   Rummy?

York   It's easy, I'll teach you, you need seven cards –

Mohammed   I know how to play.

York   Fine, I'll deal.

Mohammed   I'm at work.

York   Me too – come on – lighten up. Don't you wanna see the cards?

Mohammed   Alright.

York   Shall we make it more interesting?

Layla   Now she's trying to hustle you.

York   I am not – forget it.

Layla   He's got no money – we've not been paid for months.

York   Well, why'd ya come into work then?

Mohammed   Because it's my job.

They begin to play.

York   Can't imagine that happening back home. If people didn't get paid they wouldn't go to work.

A beat.

You folks should get paid extra – danger money in this place. It's not even safe to get up in the morning. I don't feel safe in a Humvee so what you civvies must feel like –

Layla   Your concern is touching.

Mohammed *begins to laugh.*

York   What's so funny?

Mohammed   'Drive around – not over – archaeological sites.'

Layla   Isn't that common sense? Or don't soldiers get that in their basic training?

York   Hey, we don't have things that old in the States.

Mohammed   Look, Layla! A picture of the Statue of Liberty saying 'how would you feel if someone stole her torch?' – it doesn't even come close.

Layla   Let me see.

He shows it to her.

York (*to* **Mohammed**)   We're supposed to be playing a game here. You don't know the rules at all – do you?

A beat.

York   Well, if you don't want to play nice, I guess I'll have to do it by myself

She lays out the cards for a game of patience and begins to play.

Gertrude *is showing* **Salim** *the method of logging with enthusiasm.*

Gertrude   So this is my plan: every object must have a running museum number besides its number in its particular room – the latter for making a catalogue easily usable by the public. As yet we have only the excavators' numbers, Ur 1 to 4,000, say, and Kish ditto; while objects that don't come from an excavation – like these wonderful things – have no number at all. The new arrangement will be chronological not geographical except in the downstairs rooms where all the big, heavy stone objects, too heavy to carry upstairs, will stand – a Babylonian room, an Assyrian room and an Arab room are what we begin on downstairs when the necessary fittings are made. Do you see? Tell me if it's unclear.

Salim   I understand. And this is *your* system?

Gertrude   It is. I borrowed from another I set up in France during to the war to help trace the missing and wounded. Strange there should be an overlap here – one about burying, the other digging up the past. But it's satisfying isn't it – bringing order where there is none . . .

Salim   The Assyrian kings had foundation stones for their palaces on which their achievements were inscribed. I'd suggest we had one made listing your achievements to go under the museum, but I don't think we'd be able to find a stone big enough.

Gertrude   You flatter me. I foresee that I shall make innumerable mistakes and that I shall be very boring about museums for some time to come! You mustn't let me bore the king when he comes. I can get carried away.

Salim   The king is coming? Here?

Gertrude   Yes, so we'd better get on.

They fervently return to their work.

Mohammed *watches* **York**.

Mohammed   Do you think those cards worked?

York   I dunno, but I sure like them better than the last ones.

Mohammed   Naked ladies?

York   Nope, the top fifty most-wanted Iraqis. It's hard to keep a poker face with Chemical Ali leering at you.

Mohammed   So you'd know Chemical Ali would you – if you saw him?

York   I reckon so.

Mohammed   Describe him.

York   Why?

Mohammed   I'm just interested to know what the image on the card looked like.

York   He was king of spades.

Mohammed   Is that all you remember?

York   No, he just looked like an old man, with grey hair and a moustache. He was wearing a suit and tie and his mouth was open so you could see his bottom teeth.

Layla   Sounds like a million other Arabs.

York   It's hard to describe, but I can see the picture in my head.

Mohammed   Clear enough to be sure? So if you saw him you'd know it was him, not just another innocent Iraqi with a moustache.

York   Sure. I'm not just going on the moustache thing. You guys have all got those.

Mohammed   That's what worries me.

York   I have had a whole bunch of training you know.

A beat.

What are you two so pissed at me about?

Layla   Look around.

York   The Iraqi army used this as cover – not us.

Mohammed   You just shot at it.

York   I wasn't even here then.

Ghalia *enters – she is in a foul mood.*

Ghalia   And you may as well not be here now if you just came to play cards and distract my staff from their work, they've a lot to do. You're supposed to be helping. I've seen no evidence of that so far.

York   Yes, mam, no, mam.

Ghalia   Go down to the basement and help Abu Zaman clear up.

York *goes to leave but stops.*

Ghalia   Well? What are you waiting for?

York   The basement door.

Ghalia   What about it?

York   Where is it, mam?

Ghalia   Don't you know yet?

York   I don't have a great sense of direction . . .

Layla   Oh for goodness sake, come on – I'll show you.

The two women exit.

Ghalia *slams around a bit.*

Mohammed   What's the matter? The soldier said you went to see the minister.

No answer.

Did something happen?

Ghalia   You knew didn't you? You could have warned me. It put me on the back foot entirely. I didn't have an argument ready. I suppose you wanted that though didn't you?

Mohammed   What do you mean?

Ghalia   We've only a few weeks – it's impossible

Pause.

The opening.

Mohammed   Oh that.

Ghalia   Yes that.

Mohammed   It's not a big deal, it's just a soft opening for journalists, show them we are doing something. Give them a taste that this museum is going be great again, able to rival anything in the West.

A beat.

Better than the British Museum.

Ghalia   I'm the director – I should decide when we open.

Mohammed   It's just a couple of rooms.

Ghalia   This place will be great. I believe that. It's why I'm here. But we shouldn't rush. The minister doesn't seem to get it.

Mohammed   My uncle just wants things back to normal.

Ghalia   Denying the reality of the situation won't do that. It will only put everything in jeopardy.

A beat.

But no one will listen to me. Can't you speak to your uncle, put him off, just for a few months till we see how the security situation pans out?

Mohammed   It would be pointless, his mind's made up. Besides, I think it's a good idea. Don't worry – you need to be more Iraqi about things.

Ghalia   I am Iraqi.

Mohammed   I didn't say you weren't.

Ghalia   What did you mean then?

Mohammed   You have to pick your battles here . . .

They continue to work.

Then

Gertrude *works on an article.* **Abu Zaman** *enters.*

Gertrude   Has someone come?

Abu Zaman   No. Are you expecting?

Gertrude   Nothing concrete. My mind keeps wandering from the task at hand. I'm trying to devise a clever premise for an *Illustrated London News* article. They're publishing piece after piece about Woolley's exploits in Ur – do you see? (*She proffers article.*) But nothing about this. Us. Here. The Museum. I want to change that. (*She looks at the goddess.*) If only she could talk. Give them a real story.

Abu Zaman   Maybe she can.

Gertrude   What do you mean?

Abu Zaman *holds out a hand to help her climb on to a stool so it is as if she is a goddess on a plinth.*

Gertrude   Don't be silly.

Abu Zaman   Tell us about your journey – how did you come to be in Iraq, El Khatoun . . .

A beat as **Gertrude** *decides whether to play this game. She reluctantly stands on the stool.*

Abu Zaman   I trust the journey wasn't too arduous.

Gertrude   Arduous? They put me in a bloody rucksack! Some oaf called Smith bumped me around like a common piece of baggage . . .

Abu Zaman   You seem to have survived unscathed.

Gertrude   I'm rather resilient. I am thousands of years old you know.

Abu Zaman   How is the view from up there? It's slowly coming together. Piece by piece. They're slowly beginning to understand how important this is. How important you are.

Gertrude   I am important. They set me an impossible task – an unwinnable game. Yet I'm winning.

Make a country. What did they all have in common? Not language. Not tradition. No. But the past. Immovable, intractable, unchangeable history.

A nation needs to be able to look into the eyes of the past and understand where they come from. What legacy they carry in them. And what a legacy – one of the first civilizations. While palaces, laws and complicated administrative systems were being built here, bronze age Britain was grappling with basic pottery. Every Iraqi should know this. Feel absolute pride.

Abu Zaman (*holding up a cylinder seal*)   From these small seeds mighty trees can grow . . .

Gertrude   Exactly – I need to remind them of their past – so they carry it with them into a future where this nation regains its place as the most important in the region, if not the world . . .

She becomes self-conscious.

Though – I don't think I can put it quite like that for the *Illustrated London News* . . .

Salim *enters holding a brown box as* **Gertrude** *steps down from the chair.*

Gertrude   Abu Zaman, will you order those seals for me – chronologically . . . (*Seeing* **Salim**.) Aha. How is the labelling coming along?

Salim   Like counting grains of sand. This was delivered for you.

Gertrude   From the palace? At last!

Salim *hands her the box. It has an object wrapped in paper that has a word written on it in Arabic script.*

Gertrude (*reading*)   *Melagit*? 'Not found'? What does it mean, Salim?

Salim   I don't know, Miss Bell.

Gertrude   Not from the king then . . .

He watches as **Gertrude** *carefully unwraps the item. It is a magnificent crown, bejewelled and breath-taking. They both stare in wonder.*

Gertrude   Look at this crown, Salim . . . it's beautiful! Magical!

Salim   It is, Miss Bell.

Gertrude   And someone just brought it here, handed it in, just like that.

Salim   This is where it belongs.

Gertrude   What wonderful people. What a place. Anywhere else they'd have kept it – but not here.

Salim   If they'd kept it it would have come back later, another time. Everything eventually ends up in its rightful place, don't you think?

Abu Zaman *sees the crown and smiles.*

Abu Zaman   *Melagit.*

Salim   What is it, *amu*?

Abu Zaman   It's a tradition. After any heavy rain when the earth washes away from the surface of ancient mounds, exposing archaeological objects, the locals in the area surrounding these mounds pick whatever the earth has given up: *Melagit*. Beads and cylinder seals made from semi-precious stones, carnelian, onyx or lapis lazuli. But I have never seen something so beautiful as this come to light . . . These objects are considered to have magical powers, a good omen. They are meant to be a promise of marriage, children.

Salim   It's good luck, then, a marriage – how wonderful!

A beat.

Gertrude   I have been in Baghdad all this time, and Basra before that. I've travelled across the desert, been to Syria and Palestine. *Ana ahchi kl allahjat al arabiat wal farisia* [I speak every dialect of Arabic and Persian]. What's more I've seen more archaeological sites than Salim's had hot dinners and yet I have never heard this tradition. How is that possible?

Abu Zaman   There are many rituals and sayings – hundreds for each tribe. Every time someone new invades new traditions appear, we adapt, things change a little. You could never learn them all, you'd have to live through it all . . . it would take several lifetimes, being born again and again –

Abu Zaman* (*with* **Nasiya** *who speaks in Arabic*)   You'd have to live for ever.

يجب أن تعيش إلى الأبد

Gertrude   Impossible – when there are so many ways to die. Pneumonia, typhoid, bullet to the heart, drowning, suffocating, being buried alive.

A beat. She realizes they are looking at her as she is gripping the crown very tightly like she might damage it.

Abu Zaman   Let me put that back in the box for safekeeping, Miss Bell.

Gertrude   Thank you, Abu Zaman. You're like an old tree, or, like one of our pieces of antiquity here – isn't he, Salim? Perhaps you should be the next director of the museum, Abu Zaman.

Abu Zaman   Oh no.

Gertrude   Why not? You know more about these things than anyone.

Abu Zaman   Such positions are for the likes of you, Miss Bell – I'm an Arab. An 'Iraqi'. For now.

A beat.

It takes one a little while to get used to one's new hat. The most important thing is to remember what colour your hair is underneath.

Gertrude   Is that an old Arab saying?

Abu Zaman   No but it should be, don't you think?

Salim *smiles.*

A beat.

Gertrude   I'll never get to the bottom of all this will I / – won't dig down far enough.

Abu Zaman   / If you dig down far enough.

Salim   I'm sure there are many English traditions we will never understand. I can never remember when to put the milk in tea – our tea is much simpler, just with cardamom.

Gertrude   I prefer it like that.

Abu Zaman   We all drink it the same way.

Salim *mimes drinking tea from a china cup with his pinky up.* **Gertrude** *smiles.*

Salim   Shall I make some for you?

Gertrude   That would be very nice. Thank you.

Salim *goes to make the tea.*

Gertrude (*indicating crown*)   That thing may well have magical powers, it has me under its spell . . . thinking strange thoughts . . . You'd better take it and lock it away somewhere, Abu Zaman, till we can get a display cabinet that's secure enough to hold it. The broom cupboard has a lock doesn't it? It seems sacrilegious but it will have to do.

Abu Zaman   Don't worry – I know where it will be safe

He takes the box and removes some letters from his pocket.

These came for you.

Gertrude   Wonderful! Just what I've been waiting for! Thank you.

She opens a letter and begins to read. It annoys her and she puts it down. She stares into space considering the letter's contents.

Abu Zaman   Not what you were hoping for?

Gertrude   I'm waiting for news from the palace, instead all I get is requests to go back there.

Abu Zaman   To England? I didn't think you took orders, Miss Bell.

Gertrude   It's always useful to know what people want you to do when trying to make a decision.

Abu Zaman   So you can do the opposite?

Gertrude   Sometimes.

A beat.

Now

Layla *has returned.* **Ghalia** *is working on her computer.*

Abu Zaman   Your office would be cooler.

Gertrude/Ghalia   I prefer to be amongst the artefacts – that's why I'm here.

Abu Zaman (*proffering box to* **Ghalia**)   This was left for you.

Ghalia   Thank you. Who by?

Abu Zaman   I don't know.

A beat.

Aren't you going to open it?

Ghalia   Later – I'm busy.

Abu Zaman   It could be important.

Ghalia   This is important

Abu Zaman   More fakes?

Ghalia   No, an authentic seal. I'm emailing to report it.

A beat.

Imagine the hands that seal has passed through. What it's seen – an invaluable tool which was in the ground for 5,000 years, then carefully excavated, put in a museum and admired before being grasped by greedy hands and exchanged for cash. Dealers stood outside those doors with price lists of how much they'd pay on their car. They let the thugs do the smashing. And they smuggled the pieces to the States. Or Europe. It's sickening.

Abu Zaman   There are thousands of those seals out there, you can't find every one.

Ghalia   I know, but cylinder seals are my speciality – without them what am I?

Abu Zaman   A camel without a desert.

Ghalia   Exactly.

Ghalia/Gertrude   Will you set up a meeting with the chief of police?

Abu Zaman *nods.*

Gertrude   We need to ensure everything on display for this ludicrous opening is secure.

Abu Zaman   *Bil khidme.*

Gertrude *is looking at the glass cabinet.*

Gertrude/Ghalia   Thank God she's not damaged. (*Indicating the invisible statue.*) So beautiful.

Mohammed   Beautiful but heavy – I nearly got a hernia lifting her into that case. (*To statue.*) No more baklava for you, young lady – diet time.

Layla *smiles.*

Ghalia   She's very important, don't mock her!

Mohammed   I'm only joking.

Ghalia   It starts with teasing and disrespect and ends with battery and destruction.

Layla   That's quite a leap . . . What's the matter?

Ghalia   I knew what to expect here but it's still a shock. It's like a rollercoaster – you must have ice water running through your veins to take it all in your stride. Every time I see something that has been destroyed it's like a knife in my flesh. Doesn't it break your heart, Layla?

A beat.

Layla   There are bodies in the streets. It puts broken statues into perspective.

A beat.

Ghalia   Your brother. I'm sorry.

A beat.

Layla   Besides – one piece on its own means nothing. It needs to be in context.

Ghalia   Such an archaeologist.

Mohammed   You're both archaeologists.

Woolley *enters and looks at the statue in the cabinet.*

Woolley   There she is.

Ghalia   But Layla is a purist – she believes artefacts should be left where they are found, experienced in that context. Taking them out of the ground is probably a step too far.

Mohammed   *What*?

Layla   Well, it's too late now – they *have* been dug up. But they won't survive. Gradually eroding –

Woolley   I'm not sure she's happy here.

Gertrude (*indicating glass cabinet*)   It's where she belongs.

Layla   Now they're above ground they should be where they belong, where they were found as part of a community museum – not this globalized, commodified, Western version of a museum, shaping historical narrative in the way that suits those in power. Artefacts as trophies.

Mohammed   I love it when she gets all academic.

Woolley   She'd look better in a nice secure display cabinet at the British Museum. I'm glad you got her back in one piece. I heard Smith carried her in a rucksack.

Gertrude   That's a lot of tosh. You should not listen to rumours, Len – she was carefully wrapped in a trunk. I wouldn't be so careless.

Woolley   Who'll see her here though, eh? Goddesses are for worshipping.

Ghalia   You'd prefer to leave them in harm's way? No. She should be locked in the basement where she will be safe and secure.

Mohammed   Next you'll say she should be back at the British Museum. But people must see her – *here*. We want this to be a tourist destination! Change the way people think about Iraq! Layla – help me.

Layla   Help you?

Woolley   Let me take her to safety.

Mohammed   To convince her not to lock the goddess up – we need her! For the opening!

Layla   She has no business being in Baghdad. This isn't her home.

Gertrude   It's out of my hands. It's the law.

Woolley   You made the law, you can break the law . . .

Ghalia   She's been here since the original opening, bar a loan to the British Museum . . .

Mohammed   It's amazing they ever let her come back.

Layla   That woman. She was obsessed with the Western version of museums. Too many artefacts were taken from their rightful places. Half of everything went to the people who organized the dig as payment. I.e. the West.

Ghalia   Half of it *stayed here*. She was groundbreaking.

Layla   Nonsense. What about Egypt?

Ghalia   What about Egypt?

Gertrude   Would you rather we adopted the Egyptian laws?

Woolley   Native inspectors? Nothing allowed out of the country? NO, THANK YOU.

Ghalia   Many items were ruined there because the locals didn't have the expertise to dig and preserve properly.

Layla   Say what you like – that woman was out for her own ends.

Ghalia   Without 'that woman' there'd be no museum. Gertrude Bell did everything she could to keep artefacts in Iraq.

Layla   We were better off with the Ottoman laws. Duplicates were all that was allowed to be taken then. She basically put herself in charge and shared the spoils with her mates.

Ghalia   Without Western expeditions nothing would have been safely excavated.

Gertrude   Stop staring at her and make yourself useful – check my cylinder seal groupings are right before we put them in the cabinet.

Ghalia   If it weren't for her all these things would be in London or New York or Berlin.

Layla   They are.

Ghalia   No we have a museum in Baghdad despite everything.

Mohammed   Exactly, and people should know about it, that this is the greatest museum in the world, or will be . . . if the artefacts are all locked up it's no better than under Saddam.

Ghalia   What happened here must never happen again.

Layla   I'm telling you there is much much worse than the looting to come . . . Besides, broken statues have their place too. A reminder. Attempting to mend them, make them look new is a form of cover-up.

Mohammed   Layla, you aren't helping my argument. Come on – I can get a better glass cabinet – reinforced – from my cousin in Najaf. Then she'll be safer.

A beat.

The world should see her.

Ghalia   Bring the case, then. I'll get Abu Zaman to look at it. But I'm not promising anything.

Then/Now/Later

Abu Zaman* (*with chorus*)

What if –	مَاذا لو..
There was a group of women	كانتْ هُناك مجموعةٌ مِنْ النسوة
You might call them a tribe	ممكن أنْ تُسَمُّنَهُنَّ قبيلةٌ
Who lived in isolation	عِشنَ في عُزلة
Solved problems	وَحَلَلْنَ المشاكلَ
Documented their findings in writings	ووَثَّقْنَ نتائجهُنَّ بالقلم
Discovered medicines and cures as yet unknown	أكتَشفْنَ أدويةٌ وعلاجاتٍ لم تُعرفْ بعد
Could hear the Earth's language understand her	يَسْمَعْنَ لغةَ الأرضِ وَيَفْهَمْنَها
Of course they needed men for one particular task	وكُنَّ في حاجةٍ إلى رجالٍ لغرضٍ واحدٍ لا غير
But in that eventuality all they had to do was ask	كُلُّ ما كانَ عليهِنَّ فِعْلهُ هوَ الطلب
Their role fulfilled the men were dismissed	وبعدَ ما قامَ الرجالُ بدورِهم ثَمَّ صَرفهُم
The women could return to their lives	كُنَّ قادِراتٍ على العودةِ إلى حَياتِهِنَّ
But soon the men grew suspicious and raged	ولكنْ سُرعانَ ما ارتابَ الرجالُ واعتَرَضوا
They didn't like being on the outside	سَئِموا البقاءَ في الخارج
They agreed that the time had come to unseat these women	وَاتفَقُوا على الإطاحةِ بهؤلاءِ النسوة
Clearly the only way to do that was to kill them.	وما مِنْ طَريقةٍ لفعلِ ذَلكَ الا بِقتلِهِنَّ
So they stole into the tribe in the dead of night	لِذا تَسَللُّوا إلى القبيلةِ في جَوفِ الليل
And set everyone and everything alight	و أحْرَقوا كُلَّ شيء
The smell of burning hung in the air for days	وبَقَيَتْ رائحةُ الاحتراقِ تَحومُ في الهواءِ لِعدَّةِ أيام

No woman survived, the bodies dumped in a grave

لَمْ تَنْجُ أيُ آمرأة وأُلْقيتْ الجُثَثُ في قبرٍ

The children they spared, and took back to their land

لَمْ يُؤذوا الأطفال، وأخَذوهم مَعَهُم الى بلادِهم

They never told them of their history

لم يخبروهم أبداً عن تاريخهم

And so those children – the girls

وهؤلاءِ الأطفال- الفتيات

Grew up into women in this masculine world

أصبَحْنَ نساءً في هذا العالمِ الذكوري

They followed the rules

اتَّبعْنَ القواعد

Because the truth about their past they never knew.

لأنَّهُنَ لَمْ يَعرفْنَ الحقيقةَ عَنْ ماضيهنَّ

Not of the tribe who had changed the world for a time

ولا عَنْ القبيلةِ التي غيرَّتْ العالمَ لبعضِ الوقتِ

Although many of these young women would often pine

على الرغمِ من أنَّ هؤلاءِ النسوةِ الشاباتُ غالباً ما يَتَحرَّقْنَ شوقاً

For what, they weren't entirely sure

إلى شيءٍ لَمْ تَفْهَمْنَه

But their feet would carry them

لكنَّ أقدامَهُنَّ سَتَحملُهُنَّ

Into the woods to a particular place

إلى الغابة، إلى مكانٍ مُحدد..

They never knew why they were drawn to this space

لم يعرفنَ أبداً سببَ تواجِدِهِنَّ في هذا المكان

But the terrible truth they did not know

ولكنَّهُنَّ لَمْ يَعرفنَ الحقيقة المأساوية

Was that their history was deep below

إنَّ تاريخَهُنَّ أسفلَ

Their feet

أقدامِهن

Burned and buried with their mothers.

محروقٌ ومَدفونٌ معَ أمهاتِهن.

Forgotten

وَفي طيِّ النسيانِ..

Then

Woolley *looks up from his work.*

Ghalia *exits at some point in this section.*

Woolley   Before I forget – I have news – from the caliph.

Gertrude   You mean His Highness King Faisal. He's sent word with you? Why didn't you tell me sooner?

Woolley   Slipped my mind.

Gertrude   I've been expecting him to come and see my progress.

Woolley   Kinging is a weighty business.

Gertrude   Perhaps he wants it to be a surprise. At the opening.

Woolley   Perhaps he's busy with the ruminations of monarchy –

Gertrude   You don't need to tell me – I've sat by him and helped him draw up laws on oil concessions, medical practices, dredging the river, and more. I was intimate with every stitch of this young country's vestments. But now . . .

A beat.

I wish the king would invite me to *majlis* as he used to. I never know what's going on in the cabinet these days and I have an uneasy feeling that no one is controlling things.

Woolley   There's the king.

Gertrude   What's a king without his advisor?

Woolley   He has advisors.

Gertrude   His *English* one.

A beat.

What did he say?

Woolley   The usual niceties – asking about my dig. Very polite as he doesn't have the first idea.

Gertrude   What else?

Woolley   Talk of the weather – the floods.

Gertrude   Yes, and?

Woolley   The general strike at home.

Gertrude   Tell me what he wants, you awful man!

Woolley   Ah, yes, well, he said there's something important he wants you to do.

Gertrude   I knew it! They want me to negotiate with the Turks about the oil fields don't they – I was surprised they didn't ask me in the first place. I'll message the maid to pack.

Woolley   No, no, Gerty, not that – that's in hand. No it's about this place.

Gertrude   Oh.

Woolley   I wonder if I should tell you – now I've been here.

Gertrude   What's wrong with it?

Woolley   Nothing – but you've still such a lot to do.

Gertrude   I have time.

Woolley   He asks if you can do it by 14 June?

Gertrude   Do what?

Woolley   Have it finished –

Gertrude   That's just a few weeks away.

Woolley   He thinks it's important – let the people know we are doing something . . . that sort of thing. He will come. Cut a ribbon, make a speech –

A beat.

You'll have to tell him no.

Gertrude   Out of the question.

Woolley   Quite – too much to do.

Gertrude   No, it's out of the question to say no – he's right of course, it's important – let the people know we are doing something . . .

A beat.

Faisal sent no letter to me?

Woolley   No. Just the message. Open the museum. Then your work here will be done.

Gertrude   Is that your opinion – or his? Besides – it will never be done.

Woolley   Well, then, you can pass on the mantle as planned. I must go, I've a report to write on Ur for the BM – wretched white ants ate my first effort. We've all got responsibilities back in Blighty, eh?

A beat.

You really think you can do it – the 14th?

Gertrude   Len, the museum is a life-long task, but I know I can make the Babylonian stone room ready for an opening, make the king proud, remind him what I'm capable of. The rest of the museum will take much longer to be finished. Just logging these items is taking for ever, though my system is good. It's all rather Sisyphean – and the rooms upstairs look like a bomb site –

Woolley   Archaeological site surely. Let's not conjure more wars, Gerty . . .

Now

York   I've done a bad thing. I need to tell someone about it.

Layla *appears as if summoned.*

York   That mask got me thinking. The Warka one . . . that came back.

Layla   Look I'm not really qualified – you should speak to the director or don't you have counsellors at your base or something.

York   Oh not that kind of bad thing, it's to do with an artefact.

Layla   Something stolen? Go on.

York   Well, in my first week here I was patrolling on the Friday, on Mutanabi Street, and I came across the book market there, what an incredible sight, as if the street was paved with books, and cars covered in books too and people all gathered around reading – not buying just reading like they were eating up the pages . . .

Layla   They can't afford to buy.

York   I guess not, but it was amazing, all these people and they reading and these books, and as I walked I saw one guy with these beautiful maps. Maps of the Mid East with Arabic writing marking different places, archaeological sites, cities, the rivers, so decorative . . . He saw me looking and called me inside the shop. I thought he wanted me in a professional capacity – you know as a solider. I didn't think he'd try and sell me anything. But he got out this map, this amazing map. And he said it was one of the first maps of Iraq, just after it became a country over eighty years ago, that it belonged to the first king, King Faisal, and then was given to the National Library where it hung until the war. He said he could see I'd take care of it, make sure it got a good home in the States, was displayed somewhere, he didn't want it to get destroyed here –

Layla   How much did you pay?

York   Five hundred dollars . . . I couldn't help myself, it was so beautiful, it seemed like the right thing to do – to save it.

A beat.

But pretty quick I knew it was wrong, what I done. And when I heard I was getting posted here to the museum it seemed like fate – you know, I could return it. Thing is, if my commanding officer found out – well, I'd get in some hot water you know, we're not supposed to buy stuff like that.

Layla   Where is it?

York   Here . . .

She takes it out and gives it to **Layla***.*

York   I thought maybe you could take it – say it was handed in anonymously. So many things are being handed in every day – no one needs to know.

Layla   I could do that –

She is studying the map.

York   I'd appreciate it – it's been on my conscience since I bought it.

Layla   Really? After all the things that you must have seen and done *this* has been on your conscience?

She smells the map – **York** *looks bemused.*

York   Sure. Civilians don't get it, but it's different when you are told to do something, it's sort of not you, you know – even the really bad stuff. But that, that's something I chose to do, myself, I have to take responsibility for it.

A beat.

Layla *hands the map back to* **York**.

She takes out a camera.

York   What are you doing?

Layla   Photo for posterity. Then you can have it back.

York   Huh?

Layla   It's a fake.

She takes a photo and there's a flash.

Abu Zaman *holds the coin up to the light examining it for dirt, then wipes it on his clothes to shine it.*

Abu Zaman   If only every problem was so easy to solve

Then

Woolley   The question is – what's in it for me?

Gertrude   The Englishman's mantra. What do you want?

Woolley   Well, once you are open perhaps you'd consider loaning us a few items? Your goddess for example.

Gertrude   I won't lend her unless I have it in writing that she'll return: I know your 'borrowing' and don't forget the Iraq laws of antiquities.

Woolley   How could I? You and your laws, like a little girl who changes the rules of the game to suit her . . . anyway I predict it'll all be back to the BM in time for tea when civil war erupts again and they go back to their tribes.

A beat.

Gertrude   What do you think, Abu Zaman – as an Iraqi?

Abu Zaman   Maybe things would be different – better if she stayed here . . .

Gertrude   Tell you what. Let's do it the Arab way – *maktouba* – let's toss a coin for it.

Abu Zaman   Allow me.

He tosses a coin. Again he affects the outcome and this can be marked or not in production at the discretion of the creative team.

Gertrude *calls 'heads'. He shows them both the coin – heads.* **Gertrude** *is ecstatic.*

Gertrude   It's heads! I win! She stays!

Woolley   Show me that coin!

He inspects it – it isn't a trick one.

Gertrude   She stays with me.

Woolley   With the 'people of Iraq' you mean. I was sure I'd win – like I'd dreamt it before . . . Why do I feel I've been had, Abu Zaman?

Gertrude   Don't blame the poor chap, he can't control the toss of a coin –

Abu Zaman   She'll be safer *here* – won't she? Where she belongs.

Woolley   As long as the Iraqis aren't revolting . . . and I'm afraid they are.

Gertrude   Professor Woolley!

Woolley   What? It is less than a decade since the uprisings here – the Iraqi revolution – and the only way we quashed that was with air power.

Abu Zaman   You predict another civil war, Professor Woolley?

Woolley   Look around, man. The tribes are twitchy – Sunnis, Shias, Kurds, Jews – all vying for supremacy. Imagine taking an Englishman, Scotsman, Welshman and a Paddy – telling them they are one family – making them share one house and locking the door on them. Go back in a week and they'll each have barricaded themselves in a room – the English in the drawing room, Scottish in the bedroom, Welsh in the kitchen and the Irish in the latrine. And when the Welshman kindly asks if he can use the facilities the others will barge into the kitchen, devour the luncheon meat, pour flour all over the floor and destroy every plate in the house. The Welshman will be cleaning for a week.

Abu Zaman *looks worried.*

Gertrude   Ignore him, he's just a sore loser.

Abu Zaman   But we want our plates intact – our flour in the jar! What would no kitchen mean for the future of everyone? With no kitchen . . .

Woolley   No one gets to eat.

Gertrude   For goodness sake.

Abu Zaman   But if things were changed. If she (*the statue*) stays here. Educates people – things might be different . . .

Abu Zaman* (*with chorus of* **Nasiya/Salim**)

The future might be better   قد يكون المستقبل أفضل

Woolley   You can't change the future, old boy.

Abu Zaman   You are wrong, Mr Woolley. It's the past you can't change. But the future . . . we must all try to make the future the best it can be . . .

Gertrude *and* **Woolley** *regard the statue from one side.*

We are Then/Now/Later.

Abu Zaman *places the coin on the floor as before and moves to look through the glass to the future once more: a future he is hoping might now be different.*

Through it we see **Mohammed** *again (Later). Again he is older and toys with his lanyard while smoking a cigarette – on a break from his work at the museum.*

A beat.

Layla *enters; she too is older. She is holding a baby – their baby. He smiles. She hands the child to him and takes his cigarette from him and draws on it. She finishes it and puts it out under her heel, then take the baby back. She kisses* **Mohammed** *lovingly and exits.*

A beat.

Abu Zaman *is smiling – looks delighted. The change he made in the past seems to have saved* **Mohammed** *in this present.*

But now **Mohammed** *spots a coin on the floor – he bends over as he did before to pick up the coin and now a group of people who are masked enter. They get to* **Mohammed** *and grab him as before.* **Abu Zaman** *hits the glass with his hand in frustration.*

York *enters sweeping up sand – she sweeps them away.*

She continues to sweep.

Now

Ghalia *enters. She is carrying the box that* **Abu Zaman** *gave to her previously.* **Mohammed** *and* **Abu Zaman** *follow.* **Gertrude** *is writing an article in a corner.*

Ghalia   Everyone. Come here. Come on. Who knows about this?

They all look at her in curiosity.

Ghalia   It just appeared – look!

She opens the envelope to reveal the crown from before. It's from the 4,500-year-old royal cemetery at Ur.

York   Sweet lord, I've never seen anything like it.

Layla   Who from?

Ghalia   Abu Zaman?

Abu Zaman *looks blankly at them all.*

Abu Zaman   *Melagit.*

Ghalia   If 'not found' – then what?

Mohammed   All that gold!

York   Funny, you'd think someone would steal that – not return it, right?

Layla   Maybe they just wanted it off their conscience.

Mohammed   It's not exactly common is it – it'd be a nightmare to sell. Maybe whoever took it was just looking after it – keeping it safe.

Layla   You can be so naive.

Mohammed   That's my youth and optimism for you – attractive isn't it?

Layla *smiles in spite of herself.*

Ghalia   When I opened it – it gave me a surge of hope . . . despite all the destruction things can get back to where they belong . . . Isn't it *wonderful*?

Abu Zaman   Shall I take it to the basement – lock it up safely there?

York   How old is it?

Layla   Is it from Ur?

Ghalia   Yes – 4,500 years old give or take –

They all stare at it looking beautiful.

Mohammed   It's going to look amazing at the opening.

Ghalia   What?

Abu Zaman   No!

Mohammed   We have to find the best way to display it.

York   Someone could model it.

Ghalia   No, no, it goes under lock and key, it isn't being displayed.

Mohammed   This is ridiculous, you are being far too cautious. A museum needs its public or it's just an archive – dead.

Ghalia   But you *saw* the looting

Abu Zaman   They were possessed, the pounding – thuds – bangs – they broke down the door – a wave – موجة عارمة من الدمار They smashed everything in their way! We need these things intact for the future.

Gertrude   / a tidal wave of destruction /

Mohammed   No ordinary Iraqis will be at the opening, it's only for dignitaries and journalists.

Ghalia   Forget the opening, what about when we lock those flimsy doors at night – who's to say they won't break them down again?

Mohammed   You are being paranoid. It has to go on display.

Ghalia   No it doesn't.

Mohammed   Did you just come back here to lock everything up?

Ghalia   Your uncle may be the minister but I'm still the director of the museum and I say *no*.

Mohammed   I'm going to call the minister now.

Ghalia   I'm right behind you – let's get him on speaker phone. My office. Abu Zaman, come with me, back me up.

Abu Zaman   The crown?

Ghalia   It has an American soldier guarding it. Come on

The three exit leaving the crown behind them.

Gertrude *steps forward and picks it up.*

Gertrude, **Layla** *and* **York** *all look at it.*

Pause.

York   It's incredible.

Layla   Must have belonged to a queen.

Gertrude   Beautiful.

York   I want to hold it.

Layla   You shouldn't touch it without gloves.

York   Almost doesn't look real, like a costume.

A beat.

It's a darn shame . . . it was meant to be worn.

Layla   By a queen. A goddess.

A beat.

Can you smell –?

Gertrude   Burning?

York   Why don't you try it on?

Layla   Don't be ridiculous.

York   Let's get a glimpse of what it would have been like . . . what about it? Don't be a stick in the mud.

Layla   My skin could damage it.

York   What are you? Bionic woman?

A beat.

It was made to be worn.

A beat.

Come on! It survived the looting – why not? I won't tell.

A beat.

Layla *looks it at.*

York   I'll shut the door . . .

Layla *slowly proceeds to take off her head covering, revealing long black hair.* **York** *respectfully turns away.*

Layla   It's okay, you can look, you're a woman aren't you?

She unties her hair and it is loose around her shoulders.

York *takes the crown out of* **Gertrude**'*s hands.*

For **Gertrude** *it vanishes.*

She is looking around for the crown – she can't see it.

Gertrude   It's gone!

Layla   Come on then, quick.

Gertrude   Where?

York *lifts the crown ceremonially.*

Gertrude   It belongs here!

York *places the crown on* **Layla**'*s head.*

York *steps back to look at her – an in-breath. She looks incredible, regal and beautiful, like a ghost from the past. Her whole demeanour changes – she is transformed.*

At this moment **Gertrude** *sees her too. She places her hand over her mouth in shock at this vision.*

Gertrude   The goddess!

Layla   I can smell burning . . .

Gertrude   SALIM! SALIM! ABU ZAMAN!

Pause.

York *has picked up the camera which is used to log items and held it up to take a photo of* **Layla**. *The camera flashes. As soon as this happens* **Gertrude**'*s vision vanishes, and she collapses shaking into a chair, her breathing ragged.*

Layla   What are you doing?

York   I was just taking a picture so you could see.

Layla   Put that camera down.

Suddenly **Abu Zaman**, **Mohammed** *and* **Ghalia** *enter the room.* **Layla** *is affected by the crown – it's as though she's wading through sand.*

Abu Zaman   I told you – look – it wasn't safe!

Ghalia   What are you doing? Hey!

Layla   Be calm.

Ghalia   Take it off!

Layla   I am.

Mohammed   So beautiful.

Ghalia   Layla! How can you – be so disrespectful. I'm shocked. What were you thinking?

Layla *takes her hijab and leaves to go to the bathroom and put it back on.*

York   It was made to be worn . . .

Abu Zaman   It needs to be preserved – to inform future goddesses.

He takes it carefully from her, checks it for damage, wipes it and returns it to its box.

Mohammed   Future goddesses? Are you feeling okay, Abu Zaman?

A beat.

York   Did you see her – she looked incredible. You should totally display it like that . . . like a statue, a goddess . . . I'm going to help her.

She exits.

Ghalia   Unbelievable. If the staff can't be trusted to safeguard the artefacts then what hope is there –

Abu Zaman (*the truth dawning*)   What hope is there?

Mohammed   Without her hijab she looked . . . amazing (*He catches himself.*) – the crown – looked amazing . . . it was alive.

Ghalia   Where are you going?

Mohammed   To try and get a mannequin and a wig.

Ghalia   What for?

Mohammed   To display it.

Ghalia   It can't be displayed, I told you it's not safe. What is wrong with you people? Have you lived with the threat of violence for so long you are inured to it?

Mohammed   This is a museum – we can make it safe – like my uncle said.

Ghalia   None of you listen to me! Is this what I left my family in England for? It's as if you don't care what happens to these things. They belong to the world.

Mohammed   Of course I care – but if no one sees them, they may as well not exist.

Then/Now

Salim *enters.*

Salim   Did you call?

Gertrude   Just – a dream –

Layla *enters and returns to work.*

(Then) **Salim** *wraps things for storage. Once he has finished (Now)* **Layla** *unpacks and inspects them, before logging them. A sort of unproductive factory assembly line.*

Layla *photographs the items she unwraps with a digital camera.*

She continues with her work. After she takes each picture she looks at the screen on the camera to check the image – but every time she does so she has to put on her glasses.

Gertrude   I must have fallen asleep.

Salim   It is hot and you are –

Gertrude   A woman? Old? Whatever it is – don't say it.

Salim   Working hard.

Gertrude   Oh. Yes.

Salim   May I ask what your dream was?

Gertrude   It was – like a mirage. Heat haze. It's so hot – like I'm beside a blazing fire . . .

Salim   Shall I fetch you some ice water?

Gertrude   No. No I'm quite well now.

Mohammed *enters.*

Mohammed   You okay?

Layla   Fine.

They work.

Gertrude   Or perhaps I'm not . . . I imagined I saw her coronation. (*Indicating cabinet.*)

Salim   Who? The goddess?

Gertrude   Ridiculous isn't it?

Salim   No.

Gertrude   Don't tell me you believe in ghosts and jinns? I thought you a sensible man, Salim.

Salim   I believe in the power of the human mind. Even if what you saw was *not* real it was a manifestation made by your brain. Your wonderful brain is telling you something. The question is: what?

Gertrude   Well . . . there was a crown so maybe it was about the king?

Salim   A warning?

Gertrude   Not about him! Faisal is trustworthy and intelligent. The best of men.

Salim   Then perhaps she's giving you a sign about who should run this museum. Be the one in charge here. A woman? YES! You.

Gertrude   But it wasn't my face I saw. I only saw the head that wears the crown.

A beat.

Salim (*of statue*)   She is beautiful.

Layla (*to* **Mohammed**)   Stop looking at me – get on with your work. I mean it.

Salim   I too have dreamt of her.

Gertrude   You're a young man, Salim – you should be dreaming of women of flesh and blood not cold stone.

Salim   You misunderstand. It doesn't matter.

Layla   The director wants everything done double quick because of this opening. She's a tyrant.

Mohammed *still watches her taking pictures without glasses and then putting on her glasses to inspect them on the screen. He laughs at her.*

Mohammed   You don't need glasses to take the picture but you do to see the image?

Layla   Blame sanctions.

Mohammed   You blame the Americans for everything.

Layla   We didn't all have generators you know. Studying by oil lamp wrecks your eyes.

Mohammed   Generator or not it was still a shitty way to grow up. I was here too.

Layla   I know you were. Unlike some people.

Mohammed   She can't help it – she was kicked out.

Layla   That's her story. I mean would you have left – if you had the choice . . .

Mohammed   Me? No I was born in this city and I will die in this city.

A beat.

Gertrude   I'm sorry. I've offended you – tell me.

Salim   I am embarrassed.

Mohammed   The glasses suit you.

Layla *gives* **Mohammed** *a look.*

Salim   You think of me as a man.

Gertrude   Well, you are.

Salim   I am a human. And now an Iraqi. In a country of religions. Many. Mine differentiates carefully between women and men. About what they can and cannot do. What their place in the world is. But people like you and her (*Indicating the empty cabinet.*) tell me things don't have to be this way.

Gertrude   Is that your dream?

Salim   Yes. I'm afraid I do want to marry. My cousin is beautiful, kind and smart. I dream of teaching her to write – like I taught myself. Of bringing her here. To see the goddess, to see what a woman can be. That it's not new thinking. It's ancient. A legacy. And I will bring my daughter to see her. So she knows what her potential is. That she can be more. And my granddaughter. They will all find inspiration. Through these things. And they will change the world.

Gertrude   How? The only way to change things, my dear Salim, is to hide in plain sight. Fit in to the structures that exist.

Salim   They won't see it like that. They'll remake the world anew. Inspired by their past. I feel it. And it makes everything alright. Any version of life is acceptable in this knowledge.

Gertrude   Any version?

Salim   I have seen war. The uprisings six years ago. Tribes uniting. Putting religion aside and rising up . . . Only to be viciously, violently pushed down again. Thousands killed. Property destroyed. Towns annihilated. From the land and sky. Showers of bombs . . . You know my grandmother's house was hit and burnt to the ground. She lives in a mud hut by the river now. But she is still there. She is alive. She exists. She endured. Like these artefacts they remind us of our past, our future, our humanity – they're for us all, that's what matters. They must continue to exist. (*A beat.*) We should build a basement. Secure. With locks. To keep them safe. Or . . . get special strong glass for the display cabinets . . . I have a cousin – in Najaf – who can help . . . I will ask him.

Gertrude *is impressed.*

Gertrude   I want you to stay on here after the opening. Help me with my work in the museum. Will you do that, Salim? Will you stay?

A beat.

Layla   This is so boring. Inside. So stuffy.

Mohammed   This is important work. To make the museum ready.

Layla   Logging items. We'll never have a complete list, all because things were removed from where they were found by Bell and her cronies. It's much easier to keep track of things when you are on site.

Mohammed   Gertrude Bell isn't the only one who dug stuff up and moved it.

Layla   You don't understand. You've never been on a dig . . . If you think these artefacts are amazing imagine them in their context, together, telling you about the people who lived there. Ya Allah, when will I be on site again?

Mohammed   You never know, if we work hard enough on this the minister for tourism might send us to the north-east mountains in gratitude, think of it – you and me and all the treasures we might discover there together.

Layla   Would your uncle do that? Find funding for a dig?

Mohammed   Would your father allow you to go on a dig? With me?

Layla   If you'd asked me that two years ago the answer would have been no way but these days he doesn't say much. Doesn't do much . . . He's not really there.

Mohammed   Then we could go. You and me. Under all those stars. We'd feel so small we'd have to hold on to each other – sanctuary – to make sure we were real. Alive. (*A beat.*) What? No acerbic retort?

Layla   Sounds alright. The director would never allow it though. Safety first.

Mohammed   Her safety concerns are about artefacts, not human beings. I'd make sure we had an armed guard.

Layla   As long as it's not that one. She's so irritating.

Mohammed   I like it when you are rude to Americans. You get a bulging vein in your head like Julia Roberts.

Layla   The Americans want to be involved in everything.

Mohammed   I used to think they meant well.

Layla   Like everyone else. I predicted that once the cowboys came in Baghdad would become a shooting alley. The Wild East. No one believed me.

Mohammed   *They* didn't loot the museum.

Layla   No. But they didn't stop it either – did they?

Mohammed   No, they didn't. They didn't stop it.

Layla   They watched.

Mohammed   Yes.

Layla   And now they are here to help us clean up. Really?

Then

Woolley *enters and regards the crown.*

Gertrude   You're here – alone?

Woolley   Hello – where did you find that?

Gertrude   How did you get in?

Woolley   Abu Zaman – but he's gone – patrolling the corridors again.

Gertrude   He does that . . . But it's not patrolling . . . It's as though he's lost something. Like he's retracing his steps . . .

A beat.

Woolley (*of the crown*)   You know, this is very like some we've come across at the royal cemetery in Ur.

Gertrude   Don't say it like that. I didn't steal it. Someone found it and brought it here. (*A beat.*) You can't have it.

Woolley   You're welcome to it. I'm sick to death of getting out gold headdresses. There are many more interesting things coming out of what I'm calling 'The Great Death Pit'.

Gertrude   Sounds *charmant*.

Woolley   It is *incredible*, Gerty. The burial pit covers an unusually wide area – the grave itself has not yet been opened and all our discoveries have been in the wider area of the pit. But what discoveries! Apparently after the body was laid in and a certain amount of earth put back, the general offerings were laid in a shaft above the grave. With the offerings were put the bodies of a large number of people who must have been sacrificed in order that they might accompany the king /

Gertrude   / Or queen /

Woolley   / To the next world. The first object was a harp elaborately inlaid.

Gertrude   How many?

Woolley   Harps – just one.

Gertrude   No, bodies – humans, sacrificed.

Woolley   Oh we can't be sure yet. Thirteen of them were laid in parallel rows except for one which was crouched up by the harp – the rest were women wearing identical headresses.

Gertrude   But how many have you taken out so far?

Woolley   Seventy-four.

Gertrude   Seventy-four dead women, all laid out in rows.

Woolley   Not all women – six were men. Don't look like that. Imagine it – down the sloping passage comes a procession of people, the members of the court, soldiers, menservants and women, the latter in all their finery of brightly coloured garments and headdresses of lapis lazuli and silver and gold, and with them musicians bearing harps or lyres, cymbals and sistra; they take up their positions in the farther part of the pit. Each woman brought a little cup of clay or stone or metal, the only equipment required for the rite that was to follow. Each drinks from the cup; either they brought the potion with them or they found it prepared for them on the spot – and they composed themselves for death. Then someone came down and killed the animals and perhaps arranged the drugged women, and there's evidence to suggest that when that was done the whole pit was set alight before earth was flung from above on them, and the filling-in of the grave shaft began.

Gertrude   'Composed themselves for death'.

Woolley   They went willingly to a less nebulous and miserable existence – the evidence is there.

Gertrude   What about the men – where were they? Laid out like dolls in a toy box too?

Woolley   No. By the door.

Gertrude   Guarding it. Locking them in.

Woolley   That's very dramatic.

Gertrude   Did they hold poisoned cups too or weapons?

Woolley   Daggers now you come to mention it.

Gertrude   All these women are laid out neatly and you presume that means a neat – a willing death. But I disagree: death is not neat or easy. They were forced to drink that poison – daggers held over them. Then they were burned. Incinerated. Out of existence.

Woolley   Not entirely – their remains are still there. Probably just part of the ritual.

Gertrude   The point is they had no choice. That's not suicide it's murder.

Woolley   What's got into you? You are so maudlin these days.

Gertrude   Sixty-eight nameless, forgotten, dead, burnt women, that's what.

A beat.

Woolley   I'm sorry I find you in such a humour but you did call me here you know. And I traipsed – on foot because of the flooding – through rain and mud, backstreets and hawkers who followed me and pestered me trying to flog month-old papers. It's not safe out there at the moment – you can feel something is in the air, building. But I came because you asked. So here I am – what do you want of me?

Gertrude   You're right. I'm not entirely myself. I'm sorry . . . I wanted to ask if you'd help me plan this place . . .

Woolley   The question is – what's in it for me?

Then/Now/Later

Abu Zaman* (*with chorus*)

A noise	ضجيج
It starts far away – this noise	الضجيجُ يأتي مِنْ بعيد..
It could be natural	يُمكِنُ أنْ يكون عادياً
Nature	طبيعة
Rain	مطر..
Thunder	رعد..
The pounding of animals' feet – a stampede	خُطواتُ حَيوانات هارِبة..
But it isn't that.	لكنَّها ليستْ كذلكَ.. ليستْ كذلكَ..
And it's not so far now. No. It's getting closer	ليستْ بعيدةً الان، انها تقترِبُ أكثر..
It gets closer and it sounds less like nature	كُلَّما اقتَرَبَتْ قلَّ تشابُهُها بالطبيعةِ..
Less natural	حَقَّاً إنَّها لا تُشبِهُها..
And there's a buzzing to it	فيها طنين..
Like bees	يُشبِهُ طَنينَ النَحلْ..
Like drums	أو الطُبول..
Like drones	أزيز
But it is human	لكنها أصواتُ بشرٍ..
It is voices.	أصواتٌ إنَّها
Many	كثيرةٌ
Raised	مرتفعةٌ
Shouting	تصرُخ
And as it gets closer it gets louder	وكُلَّما تَقتَرِب، تُصبِحُ أعْلى
The sound surrounds	الصوتُ يطوُّق
The sounds surround	الأصواتُ تُحيطُ
And then hover	ثُمَّ تحوم
Now the beating starts. The pounding.	الانَ بدأ يَدُقّ.. يخفِق..
Not a heart	إنَّهُ ليسَ بقلب..
A thud. A thump.	إنَّما رطمَة..دويٌّ..
Singular at first.	صوتٌ واحدٌ في البداية
Then more.	
More.	ثُمَّ أصواتٌ كثيرة..كثيرة..كثيرة..

More.

Thuds. Bangs.

Heavy weight against

Thick walls. Doors.

Now a shattering.

Tinkling. Glass.

Sharp.

More thuds.

The voices raise.

Unite.

In a wave.

A swell.

A squall.

A typhoon.

Of will.

Pushing. Until.

The flood.

Dams collapse.

A tidal wave.

Of intent.

Of destruction.

Overwhelms.

Overwhelms.

Engulfs.

Drowns.

Sinks us all.

What will be left when the waters subside?

Interval.

Then

Gertrude *is working on an article. She looks up and scrunches the paper, frustrated.*

دَوِيّ..انفجارات..

جسمٌ ثقيلٌ يُزاحمُ

جدراناً سميكة. الأبواب

الآن تحطيم.. طنين.. زُجاج..

حاد..

دَوِيٌّ آخر..

الأصواتُ تَرتَفع

تَتَوحد. تُصبِح موجة

تَتَضَخَم

عاصفة

إعصارٌ:

مِنَ الإرادةِ

تَدافعٌ حتى

الفيضان

السدودُ تَنهار..

موجةٌ عارمةٌ

مِنَ النَوايا

مِنَ الدمار

يقهر

يقهر

يبتلع

يُغرِق

يُغرقنا جميعاً

وَمالذي سَيبقى بَعدَ أنْ تَهمدَ المياه؟

Gertrude   Oh this is useless.

She throws the paper at the glass cabinet.

Salim   Do you need more paper?

Gertrude   No. Thank you. I just need to know what to write in this report. They're tired of my truths. But I can't just tell them what they want to hear . . .

She starts scribbling furiously again as **Salim** *returns to his work.*

Gertrude   I know how her civilization fell. Through greed and mismanagement – the hubris of men. Have we learned anything?

A beat.

I have such hope for our British mandate here. But when I raise my eyes across the border to Syria and see how the French mandate is playing out there – it's scandalous. It can only lead to war and bloodshed.

A beat.

So then I must ask – what if disaster calls here too? It's always pounding on the doors – trying to get in. I see what could happen. And sound the alarm . . . But what if I'm ignored? . . . What will happen to everyday people if the walls come down on their heads? The wonderful people here will hate me. Will blame me. And I will be to blame. But I won't bury my head in the sand. They may not heed my warnings but I can't stop. I will tell the truth – stand and scream at the rising waters though I feel powerless to stop them . . .

A beat. She looks to **Salim***.*

Salim   Did you say something?

Gertrude   Would you do something for me? It's a bit – unorthodox.

Salim   Of course.

Gertrude   I've written something – and I can't decide if the tone is right. Would you read it out for me – and then forget everything you read.

Salim   I'll – try my best. Though your handwriting is . . .

Gertrude   Thank you – from here . . .

She shows him where on the paper and he reads it out for her. She listens and watches his reactions closely as he reads.

Salim   The Mesopotamian lands cannot fail to expand economically with great rapidity and economic development will go hand in hand with the increase of political importance. We confidently anticipate that Baghdad, with its brilliant commercial future, will in a few decades replace Damascus as the capital city of the Arab world (**Salim** *looks very proud of this prospect.*) and we conceive that our task is not only to fit it for the part which it will play, but also to order our conduct of its affairs so as to establish lasting amity . . . (*He looks at* **Gertrude** *questioningly – he doesn't understand what amity is.*)

Gertrude   Amity – friendship – *sadaqa*.

Salim   Ah. Okay. (*He continues reading.*) To order our conduct of its affairs as to establish lasting amity and confidence between ourselves and the Arab race, whatever modifications the future may bring to their political status.

But if the French exercise the mandate for Syria in such a manner as to turn the country into a French province, following the lines of their policy in North Africa and in their colonies elsewhere, it is inevitable that they will meet with armed opposition which if successful will bring their mandatory authority to an abrupt close, and if unsuccessful will develop into a long period of guerilla warfare.

A beat.

He looks worried.

Salim   I hope you're wrong.

Gertrude   I fear not.

A beat.

Salim   You are like someone who sees the future. *Fatahit al fahl* [fortune teller].

Gertrude*   / What's the point in seeing the future if no one will listen to you? /

Abu Zaman*   / What's the point in seeing the future if no one will listen to you? /

مل جدوى من رؤية المستقبل إذا لم يستمع إليك احد؟

Salim   They might.

Gertrude   I don't know – I'm beginning to feel it's all mapped out. Like the picture's been taken and it is impossible to alter . . .

Now

Ghalia *sits on her computer while* **Layla** *logs items.*

Layla   This would be much quicker if you helped with the items we actually have, rather than chasing the ones on the internet.

Ghalia *looks up surprised.*

Ghalia   You're right

She moves and sits next to **Layla** *and starts helping with the sorting of items.*

A beat.

Ghalia   I wasn't actually looking at stolen artefacts online. I was looking at photographs of my grandson. Winston, my son, just sent me some – they were playing in the park near his house in London. He looks so happy. Big toothy smile.

Layla   Winston. Good English name. How old?

Ghalia   Winston *Ahmed* is four.

Layla   Boys are nice at that age. It's later you have to worry.

Ghalia   My son turned out alright.

Layla   He had you for a mother.

A beat while this uneasy compliment lands.

Ghalia   What about your parents?

Layla   I come here for sanctuary – as a place not to think about the outside.

Ghalia   I'm sure they are glad you work here and that you have a good career. I never used to worry until I had my son but when he was born all that changed. I became a worrier. When you're a mother yourself you will understand.

A beat.

Layla   What makes you think I want to have a child like you?

Ghalia   Do you?

Layla   I don't know. Maybe I want to run a museum.

Ghalia   You can do both you know. Like me.

A beat.

Layla   You never talk about your husband – is he dead?

Ghalia   To me.

Layla   I suppose we all have things we don't talk about.

She gets up.

Ghalia   Where are you going?

Layla   To get the camera.

A beat.

You know while your son is in the park taking pictures of Winston, Iraqi parents can't allow their kids to go out and play because there are no parks anymore – there are no swings and roundabouts, slides and climbing frames, only snipers and mines, kidnappping and death. And not just for the children either – so don't tell me I'll learn about worry when I have a child. I am Iraqi. I can teach the world about worrying.

She goes.

Ghalia *sighs.*

A camera flashes and we are reminded of what will happen to **Mohammed** *through a section of photographs or tableaux.*

– **Mohammed** *smoking with the lanyard.*

– *The men entering.*

– *They grab him.*

– *The pillow goes over his head.*

Abu Zaman *watches all this shaking his head, distressed.*

Then

Woolley *enters triumphantly brandishing a newspaper* (*the same one* **Gertrude** *indicated previously*).

Woolley   Have you seen the latest *Illustrated London News*?

Gertrude   I don't take that paper. A rag.

Woolley   Well, let me bring you up to date.

Gertrude   I'm busy writing my speech for the opening and no one will accept 'white ants ate it' as an excuse.

Woolley (*ignoring her*)   The headline reads: 'Heroic Archaeologist's Military Mind Saves the Day.' It continues: 'Regular readers will be be familiar with our reports of the ongoing archaeological dig in Mesopotamia which is unearthing rare artefacts to rival treasures discovered in the Valley of the Kings. Missives from none other than the chief archaeologist Professor Leonard Woolley' – yours truly – 'have brought to light a dastardly plot to plunder the site by local Arab tribesmen. The good professor and his team were working into the small hours when they were set upon by two dozen men with rifles' – it was actually more like six but who's counting. 'The armed bandits made off with a large amount of Turkish coinage and a number of precious metal artefacts including gold jewellery. The quick-thinking professor used his local acumen –'

Gertrude   Your foreman Hamoudi?

Woolley   'to track down the culprits. On doing so he took the ingenious action of offering the men security positions on his dig. The bewildered natives agreed and Professor Woolley was able to retrieve all the purloined items as well as gaining a mean security detail. That's British military thinking for you!'

Gertrude   You didn't get any of it back did you?

Woolley   No. But they are rather good guardsmen. Oh, don't yawn at my prowess.

Gertrude   It's tedious, I'm far more interested in the writing on the cuneiform tablets you found at Kish – any joy getting them translated?

Woolley   As a matter of fact yes, but they have a less happy ending.

Gertrude   Tell me.

Woolley   They detail the rulers of Kish from 1800 BC.

Gertrude   Fascinating.

Woolley   And then go on to say that a flood came down from on high devastating everything. After that the place became reborn as Uruk.

Gertrude   Uruk – our Iraq – but we haven't had our flood yet have we?

Woolley   It's lashing down out there at the moment.

Gertrude   I mean it – nothing was swept away before we came in – you shouldn't start afresh until the slate is clean.

Woolley   There was the civil war. The tribal uprising.

Gertrude   But we dashed that – stopped it in its tracks by bombing and gassing the tribes into submission . . .

Woolley   Many more would have died if we hadn't.

Gertrude   But we had no flood – we just broke the dam, steamrolled in, without invitation – have we made a fatal error – were we premature?

Woolley   Disaster was coming – we stepped in and did what was required.

Gertrude   War. Making war was required? We're getting rather good at it aren't we? You know – after the war in Europe many people said to me over and over again that it was a shock and a surprise to them to see Europe relapse into barbarism. I had no reply – what else can you call the war? How can we, who have managed our own affairs so badly, claim to teach others to manage theirs better?

Woolley   We must go through it. And come out the other side.

Gertrude   Yes – perhaps you are right – it may be that the world has now to sink back into dark ages of chaos, out of which it will evolve into something, perhaps no better than what it had.

Now

York   You guys all want me to go but I still like it here.

Layla   Iraq?

York   Hell no! In this here museum – some folks would find it creepy but not me.

Layla   Creepy?

York   You know what I'm saying . . . the way Abu Zaman haunts the corridors – I see him when I secure the entrances every morning – he stops suddenly and stares into space. Like he sees something that's not there.

Layla   He's remembering artefacts that were taken. Where they stood. His own stocktake of the missing. Destroyed.

York   It's not that. It's . . . something else. (*A beat.*) Anyway it doesn't bother me. Anything's better than the base.

A beat.

I had to strangle a dog over there to get the fellas to leave me alone.

Layla Is that some kind of euphemism.

York *looks at her blankly.*

York A what?

Layla Some American saying – you didn't really strangle a dog?

York I had to, you know what men are like. And put a whole battalion together and they're worse than a pack of starving wolves. Well, I don't need to tell you – men are the same the world over.

A beat.

The dog was just a stray – kept coming round for scraps and Private Armstrong took a liking to him, called him Hutch or Butch, and the way they all treated that dog, like he was human – one of them. Treated the dog better than they treat some of the civilians, spoke to it nicer than they spoke to me.

Layla You killed it because they were nice to it?

York No, I had nothing against it, poor thing, but Armstrong, that's another story – he's a no good son of a bitch, if you'll excuse the expression, and he kept pinching me – every morning at breakfast in the mess I'd make sure I avoided his table, but wherever I sat – however much I tried to avoid him – every day I'd get pinched and they'd all laugh and whistle the whole pack of them. Then this one morning he didn't just pinch – he crossed the line, put his hand – well, you get the picture. So I said to him, you do that again you'll be sorry, and he was all like what you going to do, missy? And I just saw red, so I walked out of the mess, went to where I knew that old stray would be waiting for the morning scraps, squeezed him by the throat till he stopped yelping and then left the dog by the door for everyone to see.

A beat.

They all call me a crazy bitch now but Armstrong doesn't pinch me no more.

Pause.

So a euphemism is something that doesn't mean exactly what it says?

Layla Yes, it's indirect. 'He passed away' rather than 'he died'.

York Amazing, your English is real good – you know more than me.

Layla We used to have the highest rates of English literacy in the Arab world.

A beat.

York Your brother passed away, didn't he?

Layla Did Mohammed tell you that?

York He's into you, you know.

Layla He's my brother's friend. Was my brother's friend. And he didn't pass away, it wasn't peaceful – it was a shower of bombs.

York   My brother died too. Now I'm the only one left. Mom was so mad when I joined the army.

A beat.

Do you have any other brothers or sisters?

Layla   No. It's just me.

York   A lot of pressure to stay alive, ain't it? Don't want to die and leave your folks childless, they'd never forgive us.

Layla   Avoiding death in America is very different from avoiding death in Iraq. You chose to come here.

York   Where I'm from there isn't much of a choice. I'd have liked to go to college like you. Wasn't an option.

A beat.

We're the same age I think. I can imagine if we were at the same high school we might have been friends . . .

Layla *looks at her quizzically.*

York   I've done a bad thing. I need to tell someone about it.

Layla   The map? You've told me – remember? Or was it a story I once heard . . . did I dream it?

Then

Salim *and* **Gertrude** *sit and work at one table.* **Ghalia** *and* **Mohammed** *work at another.* **Ghalia** *is frustratedly sorting seals – she can't seem to get the order right.*

Salim   Are you alright, Miss Bell?

Gertrude   Perfectly well thank you, Salim.

Salim   You are breathing like you're under water – coming up for air –

Gertrude   Am I really? I didn't notice.

Salim   Yes, Miss Bell, is there something I can help you with?

Gertrude   Not unless you can read cuneiform I'm afraid. I'm trying to decipher what's on this tablet. I think it's some kind of a document of ownership, but I can't be sure.

A beat.

Really, the Honorary Director of the Museum of Antiquities ought to be able to read cuneiform! Or have the support she needs – not be abandoned by everyone. Left to rot.

A beat.

Salim   'Honorary Director'?

Gertrude   I'm just keeping the seat warm.

Salim   But who else could do that job?

Gertrude   An Iraqi I would hope.

Salim   Why?

Gertrude   Because this is Iraq.

Salim   But it is ruled by Great Britain, so an English director would be better.

Gertrude   It is ruled by an Arab monarch.

Salim   Under Britain's mandate for twenty-five years.

Gertrude   You don't think that's good for Iraq? There'd be chaos if we left now.

Salim   You are right.

Gertrude   After that we will give you independence.

Salim   Independence is never given, it is always taken.

Pause.

Gertrude (*of the cuneiform*)   This is bloody annoying.

Salim   Bloody?

Gertrude   It's emphatic.

Salim   Covered in blood.

Gertrude   It's basically the same as very.

Salim   So when the English are emphatic they cover everything in blood.

Gertrude *gives him a look.*

Salim   Perhaps you could ask Abu Zaman? About the cuneiform?

Abu Zaman *appears in the doorway.*

Abu Zaman   I am here.

Gertrude   So you are. I do wish you'd stop appearing out of thin air like that. And looking so grumpy – I told you I'm not happy about the opening either – I had to pretend I was all for it, but it's not my choice.

Abu Zaman   It will be hard to keep things safe.

Gertrude   I know that – what can I do? No one listens to me anymore.

A beat.

Abu Zaman   May I see that tablet?

She hands it to him, grudgingly.

Abu Zaman   It's a document listing all a farmer's assets – and what taxes he owes.

Gertrude   A balance sheet! I knew it! Imagine if everyone in the West knew, civilization started here: bureaucracy, documentation, administration, in what they consider to be a barbaric land, that would show them in Kensington and Chelsea.

Abu Zaman   If I can have twenty minutes with it, then I can write you a translation.

Gertrude   Thank you.

Abu Zaman   *Bil Khidme.*

Salim   What is it like in your Kensington and Chelsea? Does it rain all day long. Is there green grass on all the rooftops?

Gertrude   It certainly rains.

Salim   Do you miss it?

Gertrude   England? Grey London skies? No.

Salim   Your family, your home?

Gertrude   Home . . . It's complicated. Isn't it. And when you don't see a place every day you notice the little changes. The paint coming off the walls. Tarnished cutlery. Slates off the roof. If you were there every day you wouldn't notice, because it's gradual, this eroding. But in my memory it is all as it was – all perfect. And they're all there. Even the ones that are dead.

Salim   Your brother? He died?

She nods curtly.

Gertrude   So it's rather disconcerting to go back and find things different.

A beat.

Not the routine. That stays the same: callers at eleven, lunch at twelve, dinner at seven, then cards and inane chat in the library. But everything else is wrinkled, fraying, old. People who were indispensable are missing. Gone. The cabinet's empty. Like an unloved exhibit. Tatty. Unrecognizable. And yet they move around inside it like nothing has changed – like nothing will ever change. But it's all changed – do you see? And it's sickening . . . shocking . . . disturbing. A bit like catching yourself in the mirror and realizing how you actually look – what people see – you know?

Pause.

Suddenly she seems to wake up – realize what she has been saying and feel exposed.

Goodness, I don't have time to be chatting. I've got to finish writing my address for the opening ceremony. Please get on with the labels, Salim.

Salim   All will be well, Miss Bell.

Ghalia   This is a disaster.

Mohammed   *Ya wash, ya wash!*

Gertrude   You Arabs – you're always so optimistic. / I have two weeks in which to make this place presentable for the opening. We have no glass for the cabinets – yes I know, your cousin in Najaf, but that remains to be seen – we've intermittent electricity, not enough fans, and the security arrangements are insufficient. It's a disaster.

She sets to writing her opening speech.

Ghalia   / I have two weeks in which to make this place presentable for the opening. We have no glass for the cabinets – yes I know, your cousin in Najaf, but that remains to be seen – we've intermittent electricity, no air conditioning, and the security arrangements are insufficient. It's a disaster. /

Mohammed   You need to be more Iraqi about things.

Ghalia   I am Iraqi! And I came back to Iraq thinking I could make a difference, but we aren't making any progress. Every day I learn about something else that has been destroyed or stolen – everyone's trying to blame it on the Kuwaitis – revenge – that would be understandable but it wasn't them, or the Jews as some would have us believe, it was Iraqis. And this place is for them, for us – to remind us of our humanity, our shared culture, this was the cradle of civilization and now look at it, it's like a child beating its grandparent – wrong. How can we trust them? But if we don't open this museum to the public what is the point of it? How can we move forward? But it's not safe. And now all the academics are being murdered. You know this morning when I came into work my driver stopped at traffic lights, a man knocked on the window and for a moment I was sure, 100 per cent sure that I wouldn't get here, to the museum. I'd never see the Warka vase or the lady of Uruk again. Hold a seal between my fingers. Kiss my grandson. I was going to be shot in the head because I'm an academic, because I'm a woman who doesn't cover, because they think I'm pro-America or because I work here. And as the man raised his hand he had a copy of the paper – that's all he was doing selling, a month-old paper. And my life flashed before my eyes. So forgive me if I'm a little 'irritable', but I imagined myself back on digs in the desert, discovering new things, not stuck in this airless box with you, fearing for my life. It makes me long for a grey London sky. There I said it. I'd rather be – (*She stops herself.*)

There is a camera flash . . .

Then

Gertrude *reads over what she has written so far – the first part is her rehearsing but by the end we have melted into the actual opening.*

Gertrude   A hundred years ago the first photograph was taken. That was when we humans became able to capture moments. Things. Preserving them. Holding them for ever in time and space. I've always enjoyed taking photographs on my travels. As a reminder. A way of stopping time. Until I discovered archaeology. You all know I love to travel. Especially in this part of the world. But with archaeology I discovered *time travel*. The ability to travel back to the distant past. Find out the truth about how things were then, in order to better understand how they function now. And with that knowledge I truly believe we can overcome divides and create nations, what was broken can be healed – united.

This is the true power of archaeology.

There is a round of applause . . .

Then/Now/Later

Dignitaries from 1926 and modern day mill about the space. There is the necessary mingling. We are back at the museum opening.

There are three ribbons, three pairs of scissors, three important people.

Each important person cuts their ribbon.

Important people   I officially open this museum.

Abu Zaman* (*with chorus made up of* **Nasiya, Ghalia, Layla**)   Again.   مرة أخرى

People clap, then walk about the space looking at the items on display.

Off-centre is the crown in a raised glass box with an open top.

Abu Zaman *stands close to it.*

Gertrude   Why are you standing here?

Abu Zaman   I'm just watching.

Gertrude   You're like a bundle of nerves! Anyone would think you know disaster is coming.

Abu Zaman   If it is I want to be ready – I'm here to try and prevent anything bad happening . . . to the artefacts . . . the people . . .

Gertrude   Well, you can do that from the corner of the room. Go on. There are some wealthy Americans here who might donate – I don't want you putting them off.

Abu Zaman *reluctantly begins to move to the corner of the room but continues to watch proceedings nervously.*

Ghalia   Where's the minister?

Salim   Where's the king?

Abu Zaman   I haven't seen him.

Ghalia   It's disgraceful he's not here.

Gertrude   He'll be here.

Ghalia/Gertrude   He's the one who was so excited to have it all on show.

Abu Zaman   The prime minister's here.

Salim (*to* **Gertrude**)   Are you very proud? You should be.

Ghalia *approaches* **Layla** *and* **Mohammed**.

Ghalia   You're drinking champagne.

Layla   I thought I should try it. Who knows when I'll get another chance?

Mohammed   Do you like it?

Layla   It's fizzy.

Ghalia   But your hijab?

Layla   Plenty of Muslims drink.

Ghalia   Not Muslims who wear hijabs.

Layla   I feel safer wearing a hijab. I was going to suggest you put one on. It might make you feel more . . . at ease.

Gertrude (*to* **Woolley**)   Now what do you make of it?

Woolley   Compelling speech. But these are hardly the 'people of Iraq' you keep talking about, dignitaries and military personnel and such.

Gertrude   Heathens to a man. They've barely looked at the goddess and she won't be here for long thanks to you.

Woolley   I'm only borrowing her. Don't look so glum – you've done sterling work.

Gertrude   I'm not finished yet.

Ghalia (*to* **Mohammed**)   Have you seen the minister?

Layla   No.

Ghalia   I can't believe he's not here.

Layla   The prime minister's here though.

Mohammed   My uncle's probably just on Baghdad time.

Ghalia   After the fuss he made about this opening.

Layla   Relax. Try one of these –

Ghalia   I wanted to try and convince him to put everything in storage until the time is right.

A beat.

Mohammed!

Mohammed   All right, all right, I'll go call him.

Woolley   Well, you did it.

Gertrude   I told you I would.

Woolley   It's wonderful – wonderful ancient history – but you need to look to the future now, Gertie. Make plans . . .

Gertrude   I've still a lot to do here.

Woolley   Here? You intend to stay on? We're not getting any younger, you and I . . .

Gertrude   Are you going to be giving up on digs then? Take a desk job at the BM? No. I didn't think so.

A beat.

Abu Zaman   It's all on display – the crown, the goddess, I didn't think you'd allow it.

Gertrude/Ghalia   They assure me it's safe . . .

Abu Zaman (*to* **Ghalia**)   We know otherwise – I told you what I saw. The looting . . . showers of bombs, bodies. And there's worse. What's to come. What will happen next.

Ghalia   I've tried –

Abu Zaman   What's the point of knowing the future if no one will listen to you?

A beat.

Woolley   The king isn't here.

Gertrude   He'll be here. Baghdad time.

Woolley   I'll never forget the first lecture I gave in this country. You and he in the front row – you whispering madly, translating every word. You seemed so close then . . .

Gertrude   We're close now.

Woolley   Really? Then where is he?

Gertrude   He'll be here.

Ghalia   I didn't come back to be a guard dog.

Abu Zaman   That's my job.

An Iraqi woman – **Nasiya** *– who could be from any time stands close to the glass box with the crown in it.*

Ghalia   Who is she? She's standing very close to the crown . . .

Abu Zaman   Shall I talk to her?

Ghalia   No – it's okay, I will

She approaches the woman.

Abu Zaman *gets out his coin and fidgets with it anxiously.*

Woolley   Do think seriously about what you should do next, Gertie. You've lots of options – perhaps you've done your bit here.

Gertrude   'Here' the museum?

Woolley   'Here' Iraq – perhaps it's time to go home.

Gertrude   And where exactly is that?

Woolley   Not this ferocious, dangerous place where even the weather kills . . .

A beat.

Gertrude   Do you know who I am? I've charted deserts, negotiated with sheikhs, crowned a king and made a country.

Woolley   I know all this.

Gertrude   Then don't talk to me of ferocious weather. This is my place.

Ghalia (*to the woman, indicating the space the antiquities*)   Which is your favourite?

A beat.

No answer.

Gertrude   You've always resented my position here, haven't you? My power to decide what stays and what goes.

Ghalia   I know you shouldn't be here, but I won't say anything if you are enjoying the exhibits. After all it is all yours.

Nasiya   What do you mean?

Woolley   I've always respected your decisions, but it's time now. Your family need you at home – they're all mourning.

Gertrude   Who's put you up to this? My father?

Woolley   We're just worried.

Gertrude   Who? The BM? The Foreign Office? The king? What are you all afraid of? That I'm a woman alone?

Woolley   You're not a woman – you're more than that.

Gertrude   There's nothing more than that.

A beat.

Ghalia   All of this – it belongs to you, every Iraqi. It's our heritage.

Woolley   You're working so hard – you've barely even mentioned your brother's death, never mind shedding a tear!

Gertrude   My health, my family, well, that's none of your damn business. You wouldn't bring it up if I were a man – would you?

A beat.

Nasiya   You are Iraqi?

Ghalia   Yes.

Nasiya   Your accent sounds Lebanese.

Ghalia   I spent some time in Paris . . . France.

Nasiya   I know where Paris is. You are very pale. Where do you call home?

Ghalia   Here, Baghdad.

Nasiya   Really?

Ghalia   Really. I came back to make a difference to change the future for these things. I'm doing what is right. Being where I'm needed.

Gertrude   This is about my responsibility. Doing what is right. Being where I'm needed. I've started a job and I must finish it. I owe it to the people of Iraq.

Woolley   Stop talking about the people of Iraq – what do you know of the everyday people, how they live?

Gertrude   Plenty. I've a boy working here – Salim – he tells me.

Woolley   Does he tell you the people don't want us here? They want us to give them back what's theirs and let them fight it out.

Nasiya   You say this place belongs to Iraqis. If that is true why are the ordinary people being kept outside?

Ghalia   Only for today – once it's finished all Iraqis can come.

Nasiya   We have never been welcome in this place – it's barely been open in the last twenty-five years. You know what they used to call it – Saddam's gift shop. Not for us. Next it will only be open to tourists and students. You don't trust us after what happened, but how can you blame us? You weren't here then were you? Well? No. Let me tell you how it was:

Abu Zaman *tosses his coin.*

Nasiya   There was no food to eat, no water, nowhere was safe. They turned us into savages, the British.

Gertrude   That's not true.

Abu Zaman *tosses his coin.*

Nasiya   There was no food to eat, no water, electricity. They turned us into savages, the Americans.

Gertrude   They need us.

Abu Zaman *tosses his coin.*

Nasiya   There was no food to eat, no water. They beat us, murdered us – the state.

Gertrude   They want us here.

Nasiya   At least under Saddam we could dress how we wanted, listen to the music we liked, worship our own way without fear of what others might do. Now look at us – we are killing each other . . . they've made us animals, and while you are all in here enjoying the culture we are howling at the gates for food like dogs,

Abu Zaman *and* **Mohammed** *have noticed this increasingly volatile woman and have approached her.*

Nasiya   Look – your guards are here. I'm going – I'm going. You are all hypocrites.

She goes towards the door but as **Mohammed** *and* **Abu Zaman** *check* **Ghalia** *is okay, they don't see* **Nasiya** *slip around the back of the room, find a stool, pick it up and approach the glass cabinet with the crown in it.*

Woolley   Gertrude, the king of this made-up land's not even here. He's not coming – he never was. He pretends he's our man but he's secretly garnering the Arabs against us.

Gertrude   That's not true. I'd know. I'd have heard about these things –

Woolley   You're not listening anymore. Or no one's telling you. But you need to hear me now.

Gertrude   NO.

Woolley   It's over, Gertrude. We're going home. All of us. It's finished. DO YOU HEAR ME?

Gertrude *sinks down onto a stool deflated and broken at the same moment as* **Nasiya** *rises on the stool.*

Woolley   LISTEN!

Nasiya   We can't live like this anymore!

She climbs on the stool and puts her hand into the open top of the cabinet with the crown in it. She has it out in a flash, holding it over her head.

RAEESE AL WIZARA', PRIME MINISTER, WHY ARE YOU LETTING THE IRAQI PEOPLE ROT? WHY? AREN'T WE SUFFERING ENOUGH!

Ghalia *shouts in horror:* **Nasiya** *holds the crown aloft – it's hard to tell if she will put it on or smash it.*

Ghalia   She'll damage it.

Mohammed   *Oufil taj* [Put the crown down].

Nasiya   This is all vanity, can't you see? People are starving while you worry about dead things – these things aren't alive, they're dust –

She holds the crown in front of her and crushes it between her hands, then throws it to the floor. As she does so, **Abu Zaman** *and* **Mohammed** *rush towards her to stop her but it is too late.*

Nasiya   – but I am real – flesh, blood – I'm ALIVE – HELP ME!

They take her gently by the arms and lead her out. Everyone watches.

York *picks up the remains of the crown.*

York   Can we fix it?

Layla   It's too late.

Ghalia/Gertrude   How could I let this happen?

Then/Now/Later

Under this speech the action of **Mohammed***'s kidnap is repeated. It begins from the word 'Punishment'. Again he is older and toys with his lanyard as he smokes a cigarette.*

He spots the coin on the floor and looks at it. He is about to bend to pick it up when a group of masked men come in and run to him.

The masked men grab **Mohammed** *violently and cover his head with a pillowcase. They bind his hands behind his back and walk him forward. He stands in the middle of the stage awaiting his fate.*

Abu Zaman* (*in English and Arabic, with chorus*)

'I was born in this city and I will die in this city'	'وِلِدْتُ في هَذِهِ المدينةِ وَسَأموتُ في هَذِهِ المدينةِ '
He said.	قال
He was right.	كان على حقّ.
'Don't worry – As long as you are fine, it doesn't matter	لا تَقْلَقي- طَالما أنَّكِ بخيرٍ، لا يُهم. المهمُ العائلة
Family is what matters'	
He said.	قال
'They'll do nothing yet'	'لن يفعلوا شيئاً،
He said.	قال
He was wrong.	كان على خطأ.
'Punishment'	'عقاب،
They said.	قالوا
'Director of idolatry'	'زَعيمُ الوَثْنِيينَ،
They said.	قالوا
'Apostate'	'مُرتَد،
They said.	قالوا
He knew what they would do if he said.	كان يعلمُ ما سَيَفْعلونَ إنْ تَكَلَّم.
If he told the secrets of this place.	إنْ أَخْبَرَهُم بأسْرارِ هَذا المكان

If he told the places of secrets.	إن أخبرهم بأماكن الأسرار
Of sanctuary.	أماكنِ اللجوء.
Of hiding.	أماكنِ الاختباء.
So he didn't.	لِذا لم يَفعَل
He didn't say.	لم يَتَحدث
And they	وهُم
In this holy month	في هذا الشهر المقدس
Removed his head from his body	أزالوا رَأسَهُ عَن جَسَدِه
Unholy	إثمَّ
Removed his body and hung it from a pillar	عُلِق جَسَدُهُ على عَمود
An ancient pillar.	عمودٍ عَتيق
But his head was smiling	لكِنَ رأسَهُ كان يبتَسِم
Was happy	كان سعيداً
Because he didn't breathe the secrets	لانهُ لم يُفشِ الأسرار
And his wish came true.	وتَحقَّقَت أُمنيَّتُه
'I was born in this city	
I will die in this city.'	'وُلِدتُ في هذهِ المدينةِ وسأموتُ في هذهِ المدينة'
And he's there still	ولا زال هُناك..
Like the palm trees	مثل أشجارِ النخيل
rooted in the ground	مُتَجَذِّرٌ في الأرض
rooted to the secrets	مُتَجَذِّرٌ في الأسرار
rooted to us.	مُتَجَذِّرٌ بنا

Now

Inside the museum **Ghalia** *turns to* **York***.*

Ghalia   Where the bloody hell were you?

York (*she has a broom and is sweeping again*)   You can't blame us.

Ghalia   Yes I can – how did she get in?

York   Everyone knew the opening was happening – it was public knowledge.

Layla   At least it was just the crown.

Mohammed   My pragmatist.

Ghalia   What do you mean 'at least'?

Layla   She could have destroyed something more precious.

Ghalia   The statue?

Layla   NO – a human – living – person – you – me, him!

Mohammed   As long as you are fine it doesn't matter. Family is what matters.

Layla   We aren't family.

Mohammed   We will be.

Ghalia   She wouldn't have hurt us.

Layla   I saw you. You thought she was going to attack you. And I don't blame you. Everywhere Iraqis are killing Iraqis – and yet the military is in here.

York   Sectarianism is an unfortunate outcome to all this – but it's Saddam's legacy, you can't blame the US military.

Layla   Iraqis weren't killing each other before you came here.

York   Saddam was an Iraqi and he killed a lot of his own people. It's my understanding that's why she (*indicating* **Ghalia**) was living in England.

Ghalia   Who told you that? (*No answer.*) Well, I've more right and reason to be here than you.

Pause.

I'm tired.

York   If you don't mind me saying you look awful.

Ghalia   I barely got a wink of sleep. I kept thinking I heard the place being broken into again – by an angry mob, looted . . . But *we* were in the cases, Layla, Mohammed and I. And we couldn't escape. I should have known it was pointless to try and sleep without my pills.

York   Prozac? I'm on that too.

Ghalia   Temazepam.

A beat.

To help me sleep. I've been taking them since I got here. But a sleepless night helped me realize a few things . . .

A beat.

Mohammed (*of* **York** *sweeping*)   Don't you mind doing that?

York   Not really. It's kind of therapeutic. Abu Zaman asked me.

Mohammed   Not what you were trained for though is it?

York   Beats patrolling the streets waiting for a car to blow up in your face. Or to be kidnapped . . .

A beat.

Besides I was the only girl at home, I'm used to it. Plus here I'm surrounded by all this amazing old stuff, it's really neat. This place is like a haven, a sanctuary. Nothing bad could happen here . . . Oh.

Mohammed   I'm going for a smoke.

Layla   You should quit.

Mohammed   I will. Just not today.

He goes.

York   Did something happen – between you guys? (*No answer.*) He likes you, you know.

Layla   I know.

York   Do you like him?

No answer.

You pretend, but you're not so tough. You like him too. I can see it all now. You two – marriage, kids, the whole nine yards. He'll be the director of the museum. You'll be his right-hand woman.

Layla   The professor is the director of the museum.

Ghalia   What a job. Like having a target on your head. Mohammed's welcome to it.

Layla   He has no experience.

Ghalia   Not yet – but he's ambitious. Layla, will you get Abu Zaman for me please.

Layla *exits.*

York   She going into hiding? (*Indicating the empty case.*)

Ghalia   What?

York   The statue. Into the basement?

Ghalia   Until it's safe enough for her to be on display.

York   That's a shame.

Ghalia   Can no one hear me? Until we can secure this place it should not be open at all. I don't even know why I'm here.

A beat.

York   Have you got a dustpan and brush?

Salim *enters.*

Salim   Miss Bell, I just saw them – taking her away . . .

No answer.

Salim   Why are they moving the statue?

Gertrude   Why do you think?

A beat.

She's going to London.

Salim   The British Museum?

Gertrude   That's correct.

Salim   But you said that things that are found here belong to us Arabs, us Iraqis – you wrote the laws to protect our artefacts.

Gertrude   Yes I did.

Salim   But you are sending her to the British Museum.

Gertrude   Yes.

Salim   Will she come back?

No answer.

You said –

Gertrude   Maybe she's not Iraqi at all – when she was carved there was no Iraq was there? So maybe it doesn't matter where she is.

Salim   What is found in Iraq stays in Iraq you said!

Gertrude   Professor Woolley and I were tossing a coin and I lost her.

Salim   But you never lose.

Gertrude   Well, I did this time. Perhaps it's for the best – perhaps she will be safer there.

A beat.

When do you think we will be able to open this museum to the public, Salim?

Salim   You already had the opening.

Gertrude   Yes, yes, but I mean to normal people? Next week, next month? Next year? In ten years? 1936? One hundred? 2026? Will it ever be the right time – safe enough? Have I been premature in creating this place?

Salim   No.

Gertrude   Who will protect all this? Would you? Lie across the door if there was a braying mob trying to get in? Risk your life?

A beat.

What would you risk you life for? The statue? The museum? Well?

Salim   My cousin. I'd put myself in front of her. To save her. And you?

Gertrude   I'm too old. Powerless now.

Salim   That's an excuse!

A beat.

Gertrude   You are angry with me.

Salim   Yes. We need you.

Gertrude   This is where I belong. I won't go back to England. Call the car.

Salim *exits.*

Gertrude *folds a letter she has written and puts it into an envelope.*

Abu Zaman *enters.*

Abu Zaman   You wanted me?

Gertrude/Ghalia   I want you to take this letter.

Abu Zaman   You are leaving?

Gertrude   I can't change anything.

Abu Zaman   What did you say?

Ghalia   I can't change anything. I've tried. I'm powerless.

Gertrude/Ghalia   What will you do?

Abu Zaman   Stay here until things are safe – until a caretaker is no longer needed.

A beat.

Then/Now/Later

Abu Zaman* (*plus chorus*)

Maybe it is all inevitable.	رُبما كُلُ شيءٍ لا مَفَرَ مِنه
What if it is?	ماذا لو كان كُلُ شيءٍ حتميّ؟
It is	مَحْتُومٌ
What if I can't?	ماذا لو لَم اسْتَطِعْ؟
I can't	لااستطيع
No one can	لا احَدَ يستطيع
It seems	على مايبدو
Maktouba	مَكتوبَةٌ
It is written	انها مكتوبة

But not on paper	لٰكِن ليسَ على الوَرق.
Not on something so perishable.	ولا مكتوبةً على شيءٍ قابلٍ لِلتلف. قابلٍ للتغيير.
So changeable.	
On the Earth. On clay.	على الأرض. على الطين.
A clay tablet	لوحٌ طينيّ.
It can't be unwritten.	لا يُمكِنُ مَسحُه
If you throw those etched clay words	إذا رميت تِلكَ الكلماتِ الطينيّة المحفورةَ
Into the fire	في النار
They become even more steadfast	تُصبِحُ أكثرَ صُمُوداً
Unchanging	لاتتغير
Not like writing in the sand	ليسَ مِثل الكِتابةِ على الرمال
But in the stars	لكن في النجوم
The hard	الصارِمَةِ
cold	الباردة
Unmoving	الثابتة
Stars.	النجوم
Under all those stars . . .	تحت كُلّ تِلكَ النجوم
The merciless stars that will not change their constellations.	النُجومُ القاسيَة التي لن تُغيرَ أبراجها

Now

Layla   You've packed the statue away?

Ghalia   I said it to the minister, I said it to Mohammed and I've said it to you – it is not safe here. Not safe for the artefacts, and now I know it's not safe for us either

Layla   Because of that woman? Oh, it could have been worse.

Ghalia   I used to find your coldness – your pragmatism disturbing, but now I understand

Layla   What do you understand?

Ghalia   That you have to be like this to live here. You've been made like this to survive.

Layla   That's rather patronizing.

Ghalia   Is it? I don't mean it to be. I admire you enormously, Layla. You have more courage than me.

Layla   No, just fewer options.

Ghalia   I don't think so, you're a bright woman.

A beat.

Layla   You might have been wasting your time you know. (*A beat.*) Putting her away. The minister will decide whether we store her or put her on display.

Ghalia   I know.

Layla   You've packed up your computer.

Ghalia   I'm going. Home, to my family.

Layla   To England. Just like that?

Ghalia   No, not just like that. I've tried but I can't work in this environment.

Layla   What happened to 'This is our country and we have to protect it'.

Ghalia   I came thinking about the artefacts, I'm leaving thinking about the people.

Layla   You are afraid?

Ghalia   Yes. Yes as a matter of fact I am.

A beat.

Layla   We all are.

A beat.

I suppose everyone who can leave will leave eventually, one way or another. The British Empire did, eventually the Americans will, and whoever – whatever – comes next – whatever fresh hell awaits us here – once they've done their worst they too will leave, that will also pass. So you might as well go too.

Ghalia   You are angry with me.

Layla   Yes. We need you.

Ghalia   I can't, I'm not strong enough. I can't do this anymore just to prove something. I love my son, my grandson. Maybe Mohammed's right, maybe I'm not enough of an Iraqi to be able to withstand this place. It killed Gertrude Bell, I don't want it to kill me.

Layla   No, Gertrude Bell chose to kill herself, and you are choosing to leave.

Ghalia   And what do you choose, Layla? You have options too . . .

Layla   No I don't – I don't have the privilege of choice. That's reserved for other people, not Iraqis. None of us will have a choice until everyone goes. Until then we are like dust, sand in the wind, pushed here and there by the whims of the West.

Ghalia   Aren't you afraid of what will happen when the Americans go?

Layla   Of course, but we must go through that.

A beat.

Ghalia   You are the future of this place, you'll do well.

She exits taking her computer bag with her. **Layla** *goes and kicks in frustration the pile of dirt that* **York** *has swept up.*

Pause.

York *enters with a dustpan and brush.*

York   I just saw the director leaving. It's early – is she okay?

Layla   She's gone. For good.

York   Gone where?

Layla   Back to her family. To England.

York   Lucky her. Oh shoot, all the dust has been messed up.

Layla   Well, you better start sweeping again.

York   It's like a never-ending task . . . sweeping up sand in the desert.

Layla   When will you go back to America?

York   I don't know, no date yet, a few more months at least.

Layla   A country full of people who we don't want here and who don't want to be here.

York   I know – funny isn't it? You know what I think?

Layla   No, and I don't want to know. It's time to go home.

A beat. **Gertrude** *notices* **Abu Zaman** *cleaning his coin.*

Gertrude   Why are you still here?

Abu Zaman   Sometimes I sleep here.

Layla   Come on – you can finish sweeping tomorrow.

They leave – **Layla** *turns out the lights.*

Gertrude   I should go back to the house. But I can't face it. Another sleepless night.

Abu Zaman   Bad dreams?

Gertrude   No, too many things to . . . It feels like time is running out. Sand through the hour glass.

Abu Zaman   Time doesn't run out, it keeps going.

Gertrude   I'd like to sleep. And see what to do – a sleep where she comes and guides me. Wake up refreshed, knowing what to do.

A beat.

Abu Zaman   Sleep here. It might help. Sometimes I feel like they talk to me.

Gertrude   Alright. Yes. I'm not afraid. You can go.

A beat.

Abu Zaman   It's time.

He goes, but not before putting his coin on the floor.

Gertrude *moves behind the glass cabinet. She looks through it trying to see what to do – trying to see the future.*

We are Then/Now/Later.

We see **Mohammed**'*s kidnap once more. He is smoking. He spots the coin on the floor and looks at it. He is about to bend to pick it up when a group of masked men come in and run to him. They put the pillowcase over his face and tie his hands. They walk him centre stage and force him to his knees. We know what will happen next.*

Gertrude *watches through the glass in horror and presses her hands and face against it in despair.*

We also see in brief fragments moments from the play re-enacted:

– **Woolley** *celebrating winning the statue.*

– *The crowning of* **Layla** *as the goddess.*

– **Salim** *miming drinking the tea with his pinky up.*

– **Nasiya** *on the ladder with the crown aloft.*

There is a building soundscape of the looting of the museum. It should mirror **Abu Zaman**'*s description from earlier. An approaching noise that swells, doors being broken down then glass smashing, items being sawed, objects being dragged, feet running, voices, pandemonium.*

It should be loud, deafening – the audience should expect people to storm the theatre.

In distress and horror **Gertrude** *climbs inside the empty glass cabinet.*

At the same time:

Sand begins to fall.

It covers the stage.

It covers everything.

Still it comes.

It covers the box until we can no longer see **Gertrude**.

We just see sand now.

When the sand stops so does the noise.

Later

Abu Zaman *enters. He sees the sand and makes for where* **Gertrude** *was. He runs to that place and begins to dig with his hands.*

Abu Zaman   Here, here! Over here! Come!

A group of people come in – **Layla** *is there, but she hangs back reluctantly, unsure what they will find.*

Abu Zaman   *Yullah – bessuraha.*

They all begin to help and dig.

Blackout.

Learning Pack by Chris White

Whether you read every word of this resource pack, or dip in and out as you choose, we hope that it helps take you under the skin of a play that took ten years to make but only two hours to watch.
– CHRIS WHITE

Contents

Quotes from an exclusive interview with the playwright Hannah Khalil are featured throughout the learning pack.

Learning Pack Introduction by Chris White

At the point of writing this, the play has only had one production, one that was cut short in the year of 2020. We hope you enjoy being among the first to step inside its world, its language, its ideas, images and characters
– CHRIS WHITE

Our intention is that the materials here offer useful background and insight into the subject matter, the text and the production, so that whether you are studying the play, considering it, writing about it or performing it yourselves, you will have an ally along the way.

At the point of writing this, *the play has only had one production, one that was cut short in the year of 2020* due to Covid-19. So we hope you enjoy being among the first to step inside its world, its language, its ideas, images and characters. The play is both personal and political, microscopic and epic. It is a play about history and now, and is in itself a fleeting piece of history: *the first ever play by a woman of Arabic heritage to be staged on a main stage at the Royal Shakespeare Company.*

I first came to know the play when Hannah Khalil, the playwright, handed me a first draft in 2010 called *The Museum of Baghdad* and asked if I would read it. I did, and was struck by its scale, scope and potential, while recognizing it may take time to become fully itself. The fact that I share a kitchen, and a life with Hannah, as her husband, meant that I was in the fortunate position to read and talk about all the subsequent drafts and watch it grow; shedding and acquiring characters along the way. During the subsequent decade we would periodically meet with groups of friends who are actors in the publicly available space at the Royal Festival Hall on London's Southbank. From a building that had its own significant opening in post-war Britain in 1951, a play about the opening and reopening of the Museum of Iraq, and about the historical and contemporary connections between the two countries, was first spoken aloud. By the end of 2019, I took my seat amongst the audience in the Swan Theatre to watch its world premiere in Erica Whyman's RSC production.

At first it felt very isolating and strange seeing all these terrible things on the news and people talking about it a little bit but it was not being part of people's consciousness in the way that I felt like it ought to be.

The growth of ISIS and the destruction of antiquities, Palmyra, all of those things made the play feel ever more current and alive and gave me real impetus to keep working on it and keep trying to have it produced so that we can have these conversations about why artefacts are important when human beings are dying.
– HANNAH KHALIL

The Play

In 1926, the nation of Iraq was in its infancy, and British archaeologist Gertrude Bell is founding a museum in Baghdad. In 2006, Ghalia Hussein is attempting to reopen the museum after looting during the war. Decades apart, these two women share the same goals. But in such unstable times, questions remain about who and what this museum is for. Whose culture are we preserving? And why does it matter when people are dying?

The play is set entirely in the museum itself, and the opening stage directions say the set should be sparse apart from a large, empty, glass exhibition case. Throughout the play 'gradually more and more sand is introduced – emanating from pockets, things being moved, being swept in on people's feet'. There are also a series of camera flashes throughout the play which 'could be moments to reveal images from antiquity or the war that has raged outside'.

The action takes place Then (1926), Now (2006) and Later (this could be in 50, 100 or 1,000 years in the future)

A Museum in Baghdad addresses themes of colonialism, time, belonging and plenty more besides.

Champions of Activism Challenge: Gain knowledge, so you can impart knowledge

CHANGE AGENT

Do you see yourself or your cultural identity reflected at all in the play?

Does the play have a contemporary relevance?

What is your own relationship to museums? What do they mean to you and do you have a favourite one?

REBEL

To what extent are the characters, ideas and actions shaped by their era?

How does the play disagree with itself?

What is unfamiliar about the play that might be interesting to find out more about?

CITIZEN

Read the play again and consider the Reformer, Rebel and Change Agent Questions.

REFORMER

How are the characters changing, and how do they change each other?

Is there a particular image or line that strikes you as capturing the essence of the play?

How are characters connected to themes?

Themes

I've spent my life trying to figure out where I belong and where home is. Is it where my friends are? Is it where my parents are? Is it where I was born? Is it where I feel my heart tied to? It's a really complicated question and one I'm challenged with quite a lot so I think most of my plays deal with that too: where is home? And this play is no different from that: where do people, as well as things, where do they belong?
– HANNAH KHALIL

Just as the time periods of the play overlap and interconnect, so too do the themes. Although they do not sit in isolation from one another, there are at least three central themes – **colonialism, time** and **belonging** – underpinned by one central question:

Why do artefacts and art matter when people are dying?

Practical Challenge: Excavation of lost items – Layla/Ghalia

In the previous scene, Gertrude has asked Salim to read the speech she intends to give at the museum's opening in 1926; and here Ghalia and Layla work towards the imminent reopening of the museum in 2006.

Read the scene on **page 133**, and try the practical activities which follow to discover what else might be going on between these two characters:

- In pairs, read the scene together, sitting down, avoiding eye contact at all times. Once done, share with each other one moment that you really wanted to look at the other person and ask yourselves why that moment might be significant?

- Read the scene again, this time holding eye contact as much as possible. Is there a moment you wanted to look away or not be seen by the other person? Is there something that your character thinks or wants but doesn't say out loud?

- This time read it on your feet, walking with purpose as you speak: Layla following Ghalia. Without deciding in advance, Ghalia should find one moment to turn and face Layla. Afterwards reflect on how you both felt at this moment and what prompted you to turn at this point. If you are doing it as part of a group, ask other pairs what moment they chose.

- Switch the exercise, so that Ghalia is following Layla, again finding instinctively one moment to turn and face your partner. Does the scene feel different? Try to identify one way in which your character is trying to affect the other person during the scene.

- Now try the scene again, this time arm wrestling throughout. It doesn't matter who wins, but it matters that you struggle with each other. Were there certain words or phrases that acquired a new emphasis or strength?

- Now stand facing each other across the full distance of the room you are in. Read the scene aloud and take a step towards the other person when you feel as if you reaching out or making an offer to them; take a step back when you feel repelled by that character or rejected by them.

- Share with each other, and the class, how you felt playing that character; one discovery you have made about them, and one question you have about them.

These exercises, and ones like them, can be useful for actors and students alike to discover characters from the inside rather than judging them from the outside. In exploring the words and the situation by playing with space, movement, distance and physical contact, interpretive choices can be made and questions uncovered.

Champions of Activism Challenge: Step out of your comfort zone and make it your own . . .

CHANGE AGENT

Can the opening of a national museum help a country break free of its colonial yoke?

How can historical debt be paid?

How connected is the recent conflict in Iraq to the events of 80+ years ago?

Is history doomed to repeat itself?

REBEL

Should objects that were acquired during colonial periods be returned to the countries of their origin by the museums that are currently in possession of them?

How responsible is the former colonial power for the well-being of the country it used to rule?

CITIZEN

Can listening and storytelling between individuals from countries that are in conflict bring about understanding and the possibility of reconciliation?

Do we better understand the present by studying the past?

What are the risks of curating the past?

Is it possible to shape the future?

REFORMER

Why are objects from thousands of years relevant now?

How does the past inform the present?

To what extent are we responsible for the actions of our country before we were born?

Is it possible to create a new nation state?

Practical Challenge:
Layla's presentation to the world monologue

Refer back to the scene from the 'excavation of lost items' challenge.

- Now try the speech yourself three separate times, whatever your age, gender or ethnicity:
  - First time **rebuke** Ghalia with these words; second time **confide** in her; third time **alarm** her.
- Which one felt right to you? Could it be a combination of all three at different points in the speech? Or something else? Try your own version – if you can work with a partner, whisper the speech into their ear while their eyes remain closed, and try to create as clear an image in their mind as possible of the city you are describing. Swap over.
- Record the speech onto your phone, if possible, and listen back. Play or share the recording with another member of the group and try to identify a similarity and a difference in your interpretation of Layla.

Champions of Activism Challenge: Your agency is your superpower! How will you use it . . .?

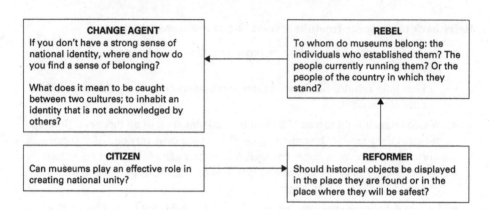

CHANGE AGENT
If you don't have a strong sense of national identity, where and how do you find a sense of belonging?

What does it mean to be caught between two cultures; to inhabit an identity that is not acknowledged by others?

REBEL
To whom do museums belong: the individuals who established them? The people currently running them? Or the people of the country in which they stand?

CITIZEN
Can museums play an effective role in creating national unity?

REFORMER
Should historical objects be displayed in the place they are found or in the place where they will be safest?

Champions of Activism Challenge: Now, change the world for the better and create something new

---

CHANGE AGENT

Congratulations! You are a Change Agent!

Your challenge is to visit a museum and find out more about an object or a presentation there that has an interesting or contested past. Perhaps it relates to your own heritage or culture. Produce a play old or new in response of your discovery.

We would love to see the results. Please send to info@beyondthecanon.com

Like the giants upon whose shoulders you stand on, you are capable of great change. We are excited about all that you shall do next.

Where Next?

Hannah Khalil published plays

Hannah Khalil: Plays of Arabic Heritage
An anthology published in 2021 by Methuen Drama comprising:
Plan D
Scenes from 73* Years
A Negotiation
A Museum in Baghdad
Last of the Pearlfishers
Hakawatis – Women of the Arabian Nights

The Scar Test

Bitterenders

Sleepwalking

Interference

Recommended plays that have similar themes to *A Museum in Baghdad* by playwrights from the global majority

Ismail Khalidi, *Tennis in Nablus*
Betty Shamieh, *Territories*
Hassan Abdulrazzak, *Baghdad Wedding*
Juliet Gilkes-Romero, *The Whip*
Vinay Patel, *An Adventure*
Dalia Taha, *Fireworks*
Amir Nizar Zuabi, *I Am Yusuf and This Is My Brother*
Heather Raffo, *Nine Parts of Desire*
Wajdi Mouawad, *Scorched*
Satinder Chohan, *Zameen*

Acceptance

Amy Ng

Playwright's introduction: Amy Ng

Acceptance was first produced at the Hampstead Theatre in March 2018, soon after the #MeToo movement against sexual abuse and harassment exploded in October 2017, so the play was inevitably seen through that lens. But I have always felt that *Acceptance* is also about finding agency as a woman of colour in a white patriarchal world. It is a play about changing the DNA of the establishment and achieving genuine diversity and inclusion. It is a play about the American Dream in the context of immigration – 'give me your tired, your poor/Your huddled masses yearning to breathe free'[1] – the promise that all human beings, *including immigrants*, have the right to 'life, liberty, and the pursuit of happiness' – and how so often this dream is tarnished, or rendered unattainable by societal forces.

2020 witnessed the resurgence of Black Lives Matter in the wake of the murder of George Floyd, as well as the birth of the movement #StopAsianHatred, in response to the explosion of hate crimes against East and South East Asians unfairly blamed for the Covid pandemic. Both BLM and #StopAsianHatred highlights the dangers of dehumanizing racial minorities, which is directly linked to the way that Black and Asian people are represented/mis-represented/not represented at all in the media, on screen and on stage. Asians especially have been almost invisible in terms of representation, except as 'technically flawless' robots or as ultra-seductive, sexually available females. In *Acceptance*, the protagonist Angela must battle against both stereotypes in her struggle to be taken seriously as a human being and artist.

In 2021, we have seen high-achieving women of colour like Naomi Osaka and Simone Bile say no to the pressures heaped on them, as they prioritize their own mental health and assert their right to live and work *on their own terms* in opposition to powerful institutions claiming the right to regulate their lives. This too is echoed in Angela's fight against the constricting life of a child prodigy.

2019–21 has also been a time of seismic political change in Hong Kong, resulting in a mass exodus out of the city. In light of the current political situation, this story of a young woman leaving Hong Kong in search of greater freedom in the West takes on new meaning.

Acceptance is set in the rarefied milieu of the Ivy League and classical music. But its themes – of acceptance, self-acceptance, forgiveness, healing and the struggle to be free – are universal. The purpose of this learning resource package is to provide context, explain the background, explore themes and offer insight into the creative process, in the hope that you will take this play and make it your own.

---

[1] Emma Lazarus, 'The New Colossus', 1903 bronze plaque in the pedestal of the Statue of Liberty.

Acceptance was first performed at Hampstead Theatre Downstairs, London, on 2 March 2018. The cast was as follows:

Birch	Teresa Banham
Mercy	Debbie Korley
Angela	Jennifer Leong
Ben	Bo Poraj
Director	Anna Ledwich
Designer	Frankie Bradshaw
Lighting	Elliot Griggs
Sound	Alexandra Faye Braithwaite

For Michael

Characters

Angelaw Chan, *student from Hong Kong, seventeen years old*
Mercy Jones, *Black British junior admissions officer at Eliot University, thirty years old*
Birch Coffin, *acting Dean of Admissions at Eliot University, Boston Brahmin background, fifties*
Ben Cohen, *Associate Professor of Music and diversity expert at Eliot University, Jewish, liberal, fifties*

Time

The present.

Setting

The admissions office of Eliot University, an elite university in Boston, Massachusetts.

The bar of a concert hall.

Music

Bach's *St Matthew Passion* is a key reference here, especially Judas's aria 'Give Me Back My Jesus' (the 'Unforgiven' aria), and 'Have Mercy Upon Me' (the 'Mercy' aria). At moments of great stress, Angela hears the arias as an aural hallucination.

This text went to press before the end of rehearsals and so may differ slightly from the play as performed.

Scene One

The voices of Eliot University applicants read fragments from their personal essays, which accelerate, crescendo and overlap, as if competing for attention.

A   I am

B   I am

C   I am

D   I am

A   I am Mexican American.

B   I am Texan.

C   I am a citizen of the world.

D   I am stateless.

A   I am British.

B   I am European.

C   I am Jewish.

D   I am Muslim.

A   I am an all-American tennis champion.

B   I am Native American.

C   I come from six generations of Eliot men.

D   I come from a hearing-impaired lesbian family.

A   My parents are Vietnamese refugees.

B   My grandmother's a Holocaust survivor.

C   My great-great-grandmother was a slave.

D   My ancestors were Native Americans wiped out by white settlers in Boston.

A   I admire Martin Luther King

B   I admire Hillary Clinton

C   I admire Buddha

D   I admire Mandela

A   I love the light at dawn

B   I love the smell of paint

C   I love David Bowie

Angela *enters. She is a shadowy figure in the dark.*

Angela 'We hold these truths to be self-evident, that all men are created equal, that they are endowed by their Creator with certain unalienable Rights, that among these are Life, Liberty and the pursuit of Happiness.' I cried when I first read the American Declaration of Independence. I cried that there were rights I never knew I possessed. All my life I had been their performing monkey, their trophy-winning child prodigy, playing Bach and Mozart on demand like so much tinkling elevator music. But in my dreams I could hear another music, something vital and urgent, bloodied, embryonic, and I knew I could give form to these charging, surging energies – if only I were in the land of the free . . .

Scene Two

November. Evening.

Eliot University Admissions Office.

Angela, *in school uniform, waits nervously. She cradles a violin case.*

Birch, *immaculate in twin-set cashmere and pearl earrings, enters.*

Birch   Good evening. I'm Birch Coffin, the acting Dean of Admissions.

Angela   Angela Chan. Nice meeting you.

Birch (*looking at violin*)   I hope you were not expecting members of our music faculty to be here tonight.

Angela   No, no, I'm not auditioning . . . I was going to a concert tonight and . . .

Birch   You're playing at a concert tonight?

Angela   No. I just bring it along. For luck.

Angela *barricades herself with the violin case on her lap.*

Birch   Optimistic to book a concert for the evening of your interview.

Angela   Sorry. I thought – 5 p.m. interview – I'd definitely make it to Symphony Hall by seven thirty.

Birch   For the Peter Sellars/Simon Rattle *Matthew Passion*?

Angela   Yes.

Birch (*half apology*)   We've been absolutely snowed under . . . I had tickets too.

Birch *takes a seat.*

Angela *hovers awkwardly.*

Birch   Do sit down.

Angela *sits.*

Pause.

Birch   Do you know why we invited you here?

Angela (*beat*)   To discuss my application.

Angela *takes out a folder.*

I brought a copy. I've also done some of the additional essays.

Birch   How diligent.

Angela   The questions are so very interesting! 'An intellectual experience that has meant the most to you.' I love that you ask not just about the experience but about the 'meaning'. I wrote about 12/8 time in Bach and the blues. The 'Erbarme Dich – Have Mercy Upon Me' aria in *St Matthew Passion* is in 12/8 time. (*Sings it, beating out the time.*) It's about Peter's remorse, after he's denied Christ –

Birch   And the 12/8 beats are the tears rolling down Peter's cheeks. We have thirty-seven thousand, four hundred and fifty-one applicants. Thirty-seven thousand, four hundred and fifty-one applications. To be read by thirty-six admissions officers. We can't possibly meet with every applicant. Do you know why we have asked you to come here?

Angela   I am honoured that you should take time from your busy schedule to meet with me.

Birch   Why are you here?

Angela   I don't know.

Pause.

Birch   There are certain irregularities in your academic career.

Angela   Irregularities? (*Pause.*) I have straight-As from all the schools I've attended.

Birch   *All* the schools. It is unusual to attend three schools in four years.

Angela   I was at the Trinity Girls' School in Hong Kong for ten years. I then won a scholarship to the Performing Arts High School in New York City, after which I transferred to the Boston Music School here.

Birch   The Performing Arts High School is one of the best music schools in the country. Visiting musicians from Juilliard, the New York Philharmonic, give lessons there. Why would an aspiring musician leave . . . voluntarily?

Angela   I want to focus more on composition. My Boston school is better for that.

Birch   We ask for two recommendations from teachers who know you well.

Angela   I have two recommendations from my current teachers.

Birch   Who have known you for two months. Why didn't you ask the teachers in New York for recommendations?

Angela (*beat*)   I am not in touch with them.

Birch   We need those recommendations to complete your application.

Angela   I'll try . . .

Birch   Is there a reason why they wouldn't recommend you?

Angela *hears the 'Unforgiven' aria and starts strumming on her arm.*

Birch   So. Additional essays. Did you try this: 'Unusual circumstances in your life'?

Angela   No.

Birch   What about this one – 'The Eliot Honour code declares that we "hold honesty as the foundation of our community". Please reflect on a time when you or someone you observed had to make a choice about whether to act with integrity and honesty.'

Angela   I am honest! I've told the truth!

Birch   Okay. My task is to pick suitable candidates for Eliot. That will contribute to our community. Because you see, every single one of our thirty-seven thousand, four hundred and fifty-one applicants is outstanding in some way. Academic aptitude. That's a given. Olympic athletes. Musical prodigies. We get them all. We are looking for Character. People who demonstrate Leadership. Who give back to Society. A Community where people feel safe. Where they can trust that their friends, their fellow students, are people of integrity.

Angela   You think I'm not – a person of integrity?

Birch   Did I say that?

Angela   So you believe I'm – a person of integrity.

Birch   You tell me.

Angela   I'm not a 'delusional liar' or a 'fantasist' or –

Angela *shivers uncontrollably and strums on her arm.*

The music crescendos.

Birch   Are you alright?

Angela   Fine. I'm fine. Sorry. If I had known I would have prepared . . . you know. Steel myself. I didn't – I expected – something different.

Birch   What did you expect?

Angela   The usual . . . Academics. Extracurriculars. What do you want to be twenty years from now? What are your strengths? What are your weaknesses?

Birch (*pleasantly*)   Alright. We can certainly do that. What are your weaknesses?

Angela   I used to play like a child prodigy rather than with real artistry. But I'm trying –

Birch   Character weakness.

Pause.

Angela   I'm not good at saying 'no'. Like . . . my roommate. She's very nice. But she likes turning up her music loud. (*With distaste.*) Taylor Swift. Beyoncé. I stuff in my ear plugs but she doesn't notice. She opens the windows, I put on my shawl, and my sweater, and a woollen hat, but *still* she doesn't see. And I – can't – just tell her.

The music is loud, frenetic and distorted.

Angela's *fingers execute vibratos on her arm.*

Birch   What are you playing?

Angela   Playing?

Birch   You're playing something specific – a phrase, a melody.

Angela   It's nothing. Autopilot.

Birch   Can you play it?

Angela   Play?

Birch   On your violin.

Angela   No!

Birch   No?

Angela   The case is empty.

Birch   You carry an empty violin case.

Angela   My violin might get crushed during rush hour in the trains.

Birch   Your case looks sturdy enough to me.

Angela   I can't risk damaging my violin!

Pause.

Birch   Let's try strengths, shall we? What are your strengths?

Angela   Music.

Birch   Character strengths.

Angela   Bach composed for the greater glory of God. But his music is a knot of suffering and beauty and violence. Sometimes I feel I'm on the verge of solving it – if I could only cut through, I would understand how to go on – how we musicians can go on. How not to give in to despair . . .

Birch   And that's a strength? I'm sorry. Are you equating your struggles as a musician with his? A man who lived at a time when life expectancy was approximately thirty. Ten of his children died in childhood.

Angela   I didn't mean it that way.

Birch   Come on. From your guts. What are your strengths?

Long pause.

Angela   I think . . .

I'm quite . . .

I can be . . .

I have . . .

Birch   You're thinking too much.

Scene Three

Next day. Morning.

Eliot University Admissions Office.

Mercy *packs up her laptop. She takes off her business suit jacket to reveal a 'Black Lives Matter' T-shirt and slips off her heels for trainers.*

Angela *enters.*

Angela   Excuse me, I'm looking for Ms Mercy Jones.

Mercy   I'm Mercy.

Angela   Angela Chan. I'm one of the applicants. May I ask you some questions about scholarships for ethnic minorities –

Mercy   I'm on my way to the march in DC.

Angela   Oh – sorry.

Angela *slumps and turns to leave.*

Mercy   I really don't know how helpful I can be. Asians are no longer considered under affirmative action. Sorry.

Angela   Oh.

Mercy   But I'm almost certain all students whose families earn less than sixty-five thousand dollars are eligible for a full ride at Eliot. You'd better double check with the financial-aid office though.

Angela   Okay.

Mercy   Even families who earn up to two hundred thousand dollars are eligible for some financial aid. Which means that most applicants can get support.

Angela   That's . . . good.

Mercy   What do your parents do?

Angela *(beat)*   They're surgeons.

Mercy *(angrily)*   So why are you looking for a scholarship?

Angela   My family's cut me off.

Mercy   Oh. I'm sorry. Why?

Angela   It's . . . Long story –

Mercy *glances at her watch.*

Mercy   I'm late for my plane to DC. Look, basically you need to prove that your family has disowned you, or that you have to stay away for your safety. Social-worker reports, police reports, you got anything in writing?

Angela   Writing?

Mercy   Like a letter from your parents disowning you.

Angela   I have an email . . .

Mercy   Good, good. So how are you supporting yourself now?

Angela   I have a music scholarship from the Hong Kong government. But it runs out this year.

Mercy   An international student?

Angela   I know it's more difficult for us.

Mercy   America First, America First. I'm British. Took me six months for them to sort out my visa though we have eleven in-house lawyers at Eliot. As for financial aid – forget it.

Angela   Oh.

Mercy   Don't despair. Where there's a will . . . Did you say music? We've got a fantastic music scholarship here – full ride at Eliot, plus funding for touring nationally and internationally – I don't know all the details but my colleague Birch Coffin runs it. Why don't you make an appointment with her.

Angela   I've met . . . I don't think . . .

Mercy   You've met Birch?

Angela   Yes.

Mercy   And you don't think – what?

Angela   I'm not applying for the music scholarship.

Mercy   Why not? You must be good –

Angela   I don't think Dr Coffin wants me to apply . . .

Mercy   She said that?

Angela   –

Mercy   I know Birch can be a bit frosty but surely. Leave this with me. Angela – Chan? Right?

Angela (*nods*)   Thank you.

Scene Four

Same day. Evening.

Mercy *has just arrived back from DC. Her 'Black Lives Matter' T-shirt is stained and her jeans are ripped.*

Ben *enters, looking dapper in blue blazer and khakis.*

Mercy   Professor Cohen!

Ben   Ben.

Mercy   Ben . . . Ben. Feels weird.

Ben   We're colleagues now.

Mercy   Old habits.

Ben   'The student repays the teacher poorly by remaining a student.'

Mercy   Quoting Nietzsche is so *undergraduate*, Professor . . .

Ben *enfolds* **Mercy** *in a big bear hug.*

Ben   Mercy Jones! You haven't changed. Sorry I wasn't here to welcome you at the beginning of the semester.

Mercy   That's alright. I know you can't resist swanning around, soaking up the applause –

Ben   Swanning? I beg your pardon.

Mercy   Peacocking?

Ben   Penguin-ing, maybe. Not many peacocks in Peru.

Mercy   Peru? I thought you were in Venezuela.

Ben   Oh. That. Completely overrated.

Mercy   But the Venezuelans are the gold standard for increasing access to classical music –

Ben   I think we do a better job in New York City.

Mercy   You've done such a fantastic job at Juilliard!

Ben   Fifteen per cent of last year's intake was African American or Hispanic! (*Beat.*) How's your wrist?

Mercy   Better. But it's never going to heal enough to . . .

Ben (*beat*)   I'm sorry.

Mercy   Blessing in disguise, really. I never told you this, but at Tanglewood I realized I'd never be the best . . . I won't settle for being a second- or third-rate harpist.

Ben   Then I'm sorry I recommended you for Tanglewood.

Mercy   No. It's good to find out early – I think I'd gotten so far only because of the rarity value – a Black harpist!

Ben   You'll make your mark on the world another way. I'm not worried about that. (*Beat.*) Work visa all sorted? They've got eleven in-house lawyers at Eliot, you know –

Mercy   Yes. I have a one-year work visa.

Ben   Did you get a room in college?

Mercy   Yes.

Ben   Are they decent?

Mercy   Yes they're great.

Ben   All your stuff arrived? Did you get Eliot to pay for it all?

Mercy   Yes and yes –

Ben   How was the march?

Mercy   Amazing! One of the best days in my life! To see this sea of Black faces, empowered, dignified, strong –

Ben   And their pale stale white fellow travellers?

Mercy   A sea of Black faces with some white froth on top –

Ben (*putting his hand over his heart theatrically*)   Froth!

We're froth!

Mercy   People were cheering from both sides as we closed in on the White House. They formed a human chain, keeping the hecklers away. We were joined by the women's march, the Dreamers' march, the trans-in-military march, a real rainbow coalition –

Ben (*singing*)   'Someday we'll find it, the rainbow coalition, lovers and dreamers and me.' Love Kermit. The voice of idealism with a sense of irony.

Mercy   This is why I came to America.

Mercy *takes out a bottle of champagne and two glasses. She pours some and hands* **Ben** *a glass.*

Ben   To your American dream!

Mercy   To the man who will change the face of university admissions in America!

Ben   I'm just a consultant to the admissions office. To the new Diversity Officer at Eliot University!

Mercy *clinks glasses with* **Ben.**

Mercy (*conspiratorially*)   Birch is just the *acting* Dean of Admissions.

Ben   Whoa. Stop right there. I'm just the new kid on the block. I'm not even sure I *want* – all these carefully calibrated personal essays with just the right proportion of surmountable adversity and positive thinking. Personal my ass! Come on! You know my truth-serum interview question? 'You have fifty grand to consume tonight – what would you do?'

Mercy   I'd donate it to Black Lives Matter.

Ben   *Consume* all of it, so no giving away to charity, no buying of property, no investment . . .

Mercy   I'd travel to the Himalayan foothills to visit a recently discovered matriarchy –

Ben   You have one night. You'd still be on the plane when your fifty grand turns back into a pumpkin.

Mercy   Oh.

Ben   Not that easy now, is it? An X-ray into the soul . . . I get such interesting answers. So what would you do?

Mercy (*beat*)   I'd spend it on an Alexander McQueen dress.

Ben (*beat*)   Seriously? Mercy! Wow!

Mercy   Oh I know I don't look the fashion type . . .

Ben   Where did that come from?

Mercy   Alexander McQueen held his early fashion shows right around where my cousins lived. In Shoreditch. It wasn't all gentrified then. I remember visiting one half-term and walking past this church and suddenly these girls came out – Brick Lane girls, tough, lesbian – McQueen loved his tough lesbian chicks, and they were utterly transformed by his dresses, like dark angels . . .

Ben   That's the second best answer I've ever heard.

Mercy   What was the best?

Ben   You don't need to escape into someone else's fashion fairy tale.

Mercy *takes a framed photo from her bag and places it on* **Ben***'s desk.*

Ben   What's this?

Mercy   Ruby Bridges. The first Black girl who fought segregation in schools –

Ben   I know who Ruby Bridges is. A bit on the nose, don't you think?

Mercy   We're throwing down the gauntlet to the Establishment –

Ben   Birch is not 'the Establishment'. She's someone we need to work with.

Mercy   For fuck's sake! Her dad's name is on this building! Just because she has a vagina –

Birch *enters.*

Ben   Birch!

Birch   Ben. Am I interrupting?

Mercy   I'll make tea.

Mercy *exits rapidly to put the kettle on.*

Birch   I trust you are settling in.

Ben   Yes. Thank you. I already know most of my colleagues in the music department, so I'm sure I'll feel very welcome.

Birch   I shall introduce you to the other thirty-three admissions officers later. We have a hot-desk system, and many officers choose to work from home.

Ben   I hear we have a record number of applicants.

Birch   Thirty-seven thousand, four hundred and fifty-one at last count.

Ben   Sorry to have left you all in the lurch for the first two months.

Birch   Not at all. How was Peru?

Ben   Fantastic. I was trying to find out how classical music can help overcome trauma amongst indigenous people in the Andean mountains.

Birch   Admirable.

Ben   It's not so different from bringing music to inner-city kids.

Birch   Yes. We are very glad to have your expertise this year.

Mercy *returns.*

Ben (*grins*)   If I can sell classical music to those kids, I can sell Eliot?

Birch *does not smile.*

Ben   I know there's a lot less financial aid available this year . . .

Mercy   That reminds me – there was an applicant. A musician. She asked me about ethnic-minority scholarships, and I urged her to apply for the music scholarship. She seemed to think you wouldn't welcome that though.

Birch   And which applicant is that?

Mercy   Angela Chan. A misunderstanding, I'm sure. I can't imagine you discouraging an applicant.

Birch   Angela Chan accused her music teacher of rape.

Mercy   What?

Birch   The allegations were not substantiated.

Mercy   How do you know?

Birch   I called the Performing Arts High School in New York City when I saw Angela didn't have any recommendations from them.

Mercy   Rape cases are notoriously hard to judge –

Birch   True. Still, she might get in on the music scholarship. We must assess the risk.

Mercy   What risk?

Birch   She falsely accused a teacher of rape, or she could be a kitchen cabinet.

Mercy   A *what*?

Birch   Full of porcelain, 'boo', and everything shatters.

Mercy   Is it Eliot policy not to admit anyone with potential mental-health issues?

Ben   I'll get the – ah –

Ben *exits to make tea.*

Birch   It is Eliot policy to admit students who will contribute to the community, not destabilize it.

Mercy   We want the best. Angela's a brilliant student, world-class musician – she's been loaned a Stradivarius by a Hong Kong bank, I mean. Wow.

Birch   Wow?

Mercy   She must be good.

Birch   *Nothing* is an automatic ticket to Eliot – not an Olympic gold medal, not a Stradivarius. Every year there are at least a dozen technically flawless Asians playing the same virtuosic pieces – the competition gets more tedious by the year.

Mercy   She doesn't even want to apply for the music scholarship.

Birch   Is that right? Well, in that case . . . Goodnight.

Birch *exits.*

Ben *enters with three cups of tea.*

Ben   I still remember the Proper English Way of brewing tea – I hope.

Mercy   'Technically flawless Asians' – was it just me or is she borderline racist –

Ben   It's an observation. You know that joke about Jewish parents making their kids learn music to train nimble fingers – you know, future neurosurgeons –

Mercy   And misogynistic to boot! The consensus amongst experts is that ninety-seven per cent of rape allegations are true.

Ben   'The quality of *Mercy* is not strained' –

Mercy   Birch knew Angela was too visible with her Stradivarius, otherwise she would have buried her under the other thirty-seven thousand, four hundred and fifty applications.

Ben   'It droppeth as the gentle rain from heaven' –

Mercy   She's completely a tool of the White Anglo-Saxon Patriarchy!

Ben   She is a product of her upbringing and class and era. It's a long game we're playing. We need Birch to cooperate. We do not need you stampeding around like a bull in a China shop –

Mercy   Full of fragile porcelain, 'boo' and it shatters!

Ben   I need you, Mercy. Look at me. Pale, male, middle-class, middle-aged. I need you for legitimacy, authenticity, integrity. The last thing I want is for you to leave the country because Birch won't sponsor you for a visa extension.

Mercy   So – what? I'm to kowtow?

Ben   Our mission is to increase diversity at Eliot. We need more African Americans, Hispanics, Native Americans, Polynesians. We do not need more Asians. They're over-represented already.

Mercy   Our mission is not to hunt down rare minorities like trophies. Our mission is to create a level playing field no matter what your race, gender or class –

Ben   Absolutely. The Holy Grail – a critical mass of brilliant minorities. But then go find them, Mercy. Don't get distracted by a case which no doubt is tragic but hardly representative –

Mercy   The assumption that any woman of colour is sexually available is very representative of –

Ben   Rape is not an affirmative-action category! (*Beat.*) Sorry.

That was insensitive.

Pause.

Mercy   Professor Cohen . . . Ben. You're too good. You assume other men are like you. The things I've seen – what I've had to put up – let's just say you were the only professor who was interested in my mind, not my . . .

Ben   Thank you. But would I dare mentor another bright young student these days? One doesn't even dare shut the door any more when teaching, or go the extra mile for a student, stay after hours, listen to them pour out their hearts over coffee or drinks.

Mercy   Women *know* when a man's being friendly or nurturing or when there's coercion behind the charm. They absolutely know.

Ben   Do they, Mercy? Do they really?

Scene Five

Two weeks later. Early morning.

Admissions office.

Mercy *and* **Angela** *are sharing a bagel breakfast.*

Mercy   Sorry it's been a while. I was on the road. I just got back from a boarding school for Native Americans in Wyoming. Hopefully one or two of them will apply.

Angela   Thank you for taking the time to see me.

Mercy   Have you got the email?

Angela (*takes out a printout*)   This is from my mother. She cancelled my plane ticket home for my dad's fiftieth birthday, and told me to stay away.

Mercy   Not enough. We need something showing a more definitive break.

Angela   I don't have anything else. They've not called or emailed or texted for a year.

Mercy   It's unfair. I know. But they have to set the bar high, otherwise any student could stage a fight with their family then claim financial support. But this means we're back to the music scholarship I'm afraid.

Angela   I don't have a violin any more.

Mercy   But . . . (*Looks at the violin case.*)

Angela   It's empty.

Mercy   Why?

Angela   The bank took the Stradivarius back.

Mercy   Is that because of your . . . case?

Angela (*beat*)   Yes. The bank took it back because I was no longer a good ambassador for their brand.

Mercy   I assume your parents cut you off for the same reason?

Angela   Yes.

Mercy   I know it happens – honour and shame and all that – but if I had a daughter and this happened to her . . .

Angela   I understand my parents. They're afraid everyone will look down on our family.

Mercy   You have done nothing shameful! You're a survivor! They should have been there for you, every step of the way. Did you have to go through the trial alone?

Angela   There was no trial. My parents refused to press charges. There was an internal hearing organized by the school. My parents did not attend.

Mercy   How old are you?

Angela   Eighteen in a week.

Mercy   So in a week you can press charges without their consent.

Angela   I don't want to press charges.

Mercy   Angela. You *need* to press charges. Stop him doing this to some other young woman –

Angela   He left for another country.

Mercy   So he fled the law. So he thinks he got away with it. We've got to name and shame him! Who was it?

Angela   I signed a confidentiality agreement.

Mercy   You did what? Why?

Angela   They said if I signed, they would help me with my visa. They said if I signed, they would keep my case confidential, it wouldn't appear on my record, it would not affect my college applications.

Mercy   And you believed them.

Angela   Does it affect my application?

Mercy   What do you think, Angela?

Angela *starts tapping on her arm.*

Mercy   You win the music scholarship and nothing – not your New York school, not the other admissions officers – can stop you from entering Eliot.

Angela   I can't.

Mercy   The other competitors won't have a Stradivarius either.

Angela   It doesn't matter anyway. Dr Coffin says I need two recommendations from my New York school. I called my biology and history teachers. But they don't dare.

Mercy   I'll sort it out with Birch. You shouldn't be penalized for their cowardice.

Angela   They're afraid of mobbing . . . of trolls.

Mercy   Were you trolled, Angela?

Angela   My diary was subpoenaed for the hearing. They got a Chinese teacher at my school to translate it. Extracts were posted anonymously on the school e-bulletin board.

Mercy   That's despicable. (*Beat.*) But listen, if you blow them away at the scholarship competition, in ten years – Carnegie Hall!

Angela   I can't play.

Mercy   Sprained ligament? You *have* to jump on it right away – believe me, I speak from experience – a specialist physiotherapist –

Angela   No. I haven't played since he . . .

Mercy   Listen to me, Angela. You've been so brave. You picked up that phone. You called the police. You accused your rapist. All I'm asking for is a little more of that courage . . . It's just a block. A – phobia. I was terrified of spiders. I couldn't even stand looking at those white flowers with the spindly petals. But the zoo ran this programme called 'My Friend the Spider'. And I took it. I won't claim I love spiders now, but I'm cool with them, I'm in control.

Angela   'My friend the – professor'?

Mercy   I'm sorry, I didn't mean – And I understand why you signed that NDA. But I need to know more, Angela. All I – all any of us knows is that you accused a teacher of rape, but he got off anyway. Which means – you know how that looks –

Angela   'Delusional nymphomaniac', 'fantasist', 'vengeful', 'hysterical' . . .

Mercy   Let's change the narrative. (*Beat.*) Who was it?

Angela   I signed the non-disclosure –

Mercy   Which arguably they've breached. Which means you're not bound – is it someone well known? I don't care who he is, he can't do anything to you –

Angela   I can get a scholarship to the Royal Northern College of Music in Manchester. My former Hong Kong teacher is now a professor there.

Mercy   You want to go to England? Brexit England?

Angela   'America first, America first.'

Mercy   Americans are fighting back, in the courts, on the streets, in City Hall, in universities – sanctuary cities, whole sanctuary states! In Britain, it's just a lot of handwringing in the *Guardian*. I was born in Yorkshire and still get asked if I'm from Nigeria. I've been here three months, and people accept me as almost American.

Angela   Almost. It's always almost.

Mercy   There were nine Black undergrads in my year at Oxford. Nine of us. Flying under the radar, trying so hard to fit in. Fucking baa baa black sheep amongst all the Oxford tossers – my tutor never discussed my ideas, just circled, in red, every misplaced comma. Then suddenly, this American visiting professor, descending from on high like Mary Poppins, and he was *interested*, he *engaged* with my ideas, he *saw* me as a human being worthy of respect. He helped me get this job. Look at me! A gatekeeper at Eliot University! I get to choose who becomes America's elite, the world's elite! I get to change the world.

Angela (*violently*)   I am not the world! (*Shrinking.*) I'm sorry.

Mercy   You have a gift. Use it. Whatever mental block that's keeping you from playing – blast through it. Upload those audition samples. Write that application. And for God's sake, don't write another mini-dissertation on Bach's 12/8 time signature. You were supposed to write about something deeply meaningful and personal – that's why it's called a personal essay –

Angela   The first time it . . . happened . . . afterwards I took the subway back to school. It was one of those open-air stations on a bridge over the road. I watched the steam rising from the manholes in the pavement below, as train after train pulled in and out again. I felt my body had turned to stone, that I couldn't possibly ever move again, except to drop down straight into the oncoming traffic. Then a busker started playing blues on the violin – so sad, but glowing, like dark hot sweet potato pie. A blues gospel, with a walking bass in 12/8 time. Like Bach's 'Mercy' aria . . . And I could move again.

Mercy   Was your busker playing a Stradivarius?

Angela   Probably not.

Mercy   QED – it's the violinist that matters. Not the violin.

The lights dim. The chorus of applicant voices start up again.

A   I want

B   I want

C   I want

D   I want

A   I want to find kindred spirits

B   I want to be amongst poets and dreamers

C   I want to work with the best in the world

D   I want friends. I want to stop feeling like the nerdy geeky outsider.

Angela   I burnt my boats. I took a leap of faith across the oceans. I laid myself wide open to America. I met a teacher. For the first time my body became a vessel of music, vibrating in my thighs, in my womb, along my spine, exploding in my blood. I was plugged into an electric current which runs through all true musicians, breathing together, sweating together, falling silent together, climaxing together. Pinocchio became a real boy. Music became flesh. (*Smiles beatifically.*) Incarnation.

Scene Six

December. Evening.

The admissions office.

Birch *is working through applications.*

Mercy *enters in a stunning evening dress.*

Birch   That's a beautiful dress.

Mercy   Thank you. (*Beat.*) It's an Alexander McQueen.

Birch   It's exquisite. Special occasion?

Mercy   I'm going to the Christmas drinks at the music department.

Birch   With Ben?

Mercy (*beat*)   Yes.

Sound of a car. **Mercy** *starts.*

Birch   That's not him. Ben's car was snowed in this morning.

Mercy   Oh of course.

Birch   He's charming. Ben.

Mercy   Yes.

Birch   Over the years, I've met many professors like him. Charismatic. With many female followers.

Mercy   About the Angela Chan case –

Birch   What about it?

Mercy   Angela signed a non-disclosure agreement, in return for the promise that her case would be kept confidential. Especially with regard to college applications. Did you know that?

Birch   I did not know that. How did you find out?

Mercy   Angela told me.

Birch   Have you been meeting her in private?

Mercy   We claim to be the best university in the world. Shouldn't fact-finding and inquiry be at the heart of whatever we do?

Birch   It is completely inappropriate to blur the line between admissions officer and activist!

Mercy   It says in *your* guidelines that 'an admissions officer should judge each applicant holistically'.

Birch   'Holistically' means from all sides. Not just taking her word against everyone else's.

Mercy   From all sides. Not just taking the institution's word.

Birch   Angela's application would have been a lot stronger if she'd written about the case from her point of view. When I saw that Angela had attended the Performing Arts School without obtaining a single letter of recommendation, alarm bells rang. It could mean cheating, or drug use, or a breakdown. I've known their college counsellor for at least ten years. So I asked her – *confidentially*. And she told me – *confidentially* – what happened.

Mercy   So if I put in a Freedom of Information Act request for Angela's case records, would you read it? For a *holistic* view?

Birch   Why are you so obsessed with this case?

Mercy   You've never been groped?

Birch   Really, Mercy!

Mercy   Oh my God. You've never been groped.

Birch   Mercy, this conversation is completely inappropriate and distasteful –

Mercy   You've never been groped because your daddy's name is on this building. But what about all those women without your privilege?

Birch   Not everything can be reduced to white privilege.

Mercy   That's not what I'm saying. But perhaps you don't appreciate how misogynistic this system can be

Birch   Oh, I appreciate it all right. I've been here thirty years. I've been *acting* dean of three different departments. Ben's seconded for one year to the admissions office. He's being paid forty per cent more than me.

Mercy   But your dad –

Birch   Father would have approved. He opposed co-education at Eliot.

Mercy   Then why stay? If I kept on being passed over I'd leave . . . Or is there no life outside Eliot for a descendant of the founding fathers?

Birch   I once hoped to be an Episcopalian priest.

Mercy   Oh. What happened?

Birch   Then I became an administrator in my father's university.

Pause.

Mercy   I know it seems unfair but – consultants always get more than regular employees. We're the whitest university in the Ivy League and Ben increased diversity at Juilliard by about three hundred per cent

Birch   And isn't it just so typical of Eliot to promote a white male diversity expert over a woman?

Pause.

Knocking at the door. They both ignore it.

Mercy (*without conviction*)   He's Jewish.

Birch   It's different for your generation. You're young. Black. Female. You could well become Dean of Admissions here one day. You don't need Ben and you certainly don't need to spend two months' salary on a dress to impress him. Don't join his harem, will you?

Mercy   I'm sorry?

Birch   Metaphorically speaking.

Mercy   I can assure you I've never felt even the hint of anything inappropriate . . .

Birch   I'm glad to hear that.

Mercy   I *know* when a man has ulterior motives, and I would appreciate it if you stopped *insinuating* – groundless . . .

Birch   Maybe you're not his type.

Knocking on the door.

Mercy *opens the door.*

Angela *enters.*

Angela   I'm sorry I know it's late but the wifi failed and the deadline's today I brought the music application –

Mercy   Thanks, Angela. Leave it on my desk. I really need to –

Mercy *leaves swiftly, terrified of losing her composure.*

Birch   I thought you weren't applying for the music scholarship.

Birch *takes the application, opens the envelope and scans through it.*

Angela   Did Ms Jones tell you – I couldn't get the two recommendations . . .

Birch   You've put down a Bach aria for your chamber music piece.

Angela   Yes.

Birch   Unconventional choice.

Angela   It's not against the rules. The violin is not an accompanist, but an equal partner to the singer. Yehudi Menuhin once said –

Birch   That the 'Have Mercy Upon Me' is the most beautiful piece of music ever written for the violin.

Angela   Yes!

Birch   And still. I don't recall any violinist ever choosing an aria for a competition.

Angela   This aria is about Peter, about mercy. Forgiveness. But there's a different one, Judas's aria, that always gets in the way. 'Give me back my Jesus!' Please turn time back, please unmake the past, please mend what is broken, please restore what I've lost – the singer on his knees, supplicating, the G-major violin solo dancing, dazzling, vicious, interrupting the singer, cutting him off 'shut up shut up shut up I don't care what you say go kill yourself burn in hell forever'. Peter and Judas. Both sinned. Both begged for forgiveness. One was rejected. One was accepted. Why is that? Two thieves were crucified with Christ. One was rejected, one was accepted. Why is that?

The music fades.

I set out to play 'Mercy', but I hear the 'Unforgiven' instead.

Birch   And you think coming to Eliot would silence the 'Unforgiven'?

Pause.

Angela   It's my birthday today. No one's called. No one sent a card. Rape is like AIDS. But if I were at Eliot . . . *Everyone* knows Eliot. My relatives back in the village. My illiterate grandmothers. My neighbours, the hairdresser, the fruit seller. Eliot's the only name which can turn lead into gold. I come to Eliot, and everyone will want to know me again.

Birch   They won't forget.

Angela   Maybe they won't bring it up.

Birch (*beat*)   Judas and Peter. One was forgiven. The other could not receive forgiveness. 'Give me back my Jesus!' Turn time back, unmake the past, mend what is broken, restore what I've lost. Judas is stuck in the past, in an endless loop of remorse and guilt. He's lost all hope that he can be acceptable again. Peter, on the other hand, abandons himself to mercy, and finds acceptance. (*Beat.*) Happy birthday.

Scene Seven

January.

Admissions office.

On the table, an opened FedEx parcel with a folder inside.

Ben   The pastors, the priests, the sports coaches – who else?

Mercy (*distracted*)   Hairdressers?

Ben   Hairdressers. Why not. The barber shops. The nail salons. Hell, the tattoo parlours. Anywhere, everywhere, I want you to spread the word. We're not just going to do a recruit and dump. No more will we accept a dropout rate of eighty-two per cent for inner-city kids. Once they step foot on campus, they'll get wrap-around support. They'll get a weekly one-on-one tutorial, like at Oxford, so no one falls between the cracks. They'll get graded pass/fail only in the first two years, until they catch up with the rest. We'll have counsellors, and community centres; the canteen will serve soul food and Mexican food – is Puerto Rican food fairly similar to Mexican? Mercy? Mercy.

Mercy   Sorry, Ben. It all sounds great.

Ben   What's wrong?

Mercy   Just a migraine.

Ben *takes* **Mercy**'s *hand and starts pressing the acupuncture point on the web between her thumb and index finger.*

What are you doing?

Ben   Acupressure. I've never felt such a blocked meridian.

Mercy *savours the moment.*

Mercy   Ouch.

Ben   Sorry.

Mercy   How come you know acupressure?

Ben   I used to date a Japanese acupuncturist. She could play the body like a violin –

Mercy *twists away.*

Ben   I know – too much information. The love-life of the middle-aged . . . She used to say, 'If it doesn't flow, it hurts.' Your energy's blocked. What's happening?

Mercy   Thanks. It's almost gone.

Ben   What's wrong, Mercy?

Mercy *hesitates, then indicates the folder.*

Ben   What's this?

Mercy   Open it.

Ben *opens it and scans through the first page.*

Ben   What is it? –

Mercy   This is the Angela Chan case.

Ben (*beat*)   How did you get a hold of this?

Mercy   I requested Angela's case records under the Freedom of Information Act.

Ben   How is that even possible? Wouldn't she have been a minor?

Mercy   They've blacked out the names and anything that could identify rapist or victim.

Ben   We have thirty-seven, four hundred and fifty-one applicants. Seven per cent of those are ethnic minorities. We have ten days to round up more. Every minute you spend on her case is time lost on another candidate. Think of all those brilliant minority candidates you could be discovering, wooing, encouraging –

Mercy   Ben, this is the case that everyone's trying to bury. If Angela had been a victim of any other crime, if she'd been mugged, or had her identity stolen, been lynched by racists, made to work in a sweat shop, deported, you would totally be on her side.

Ben   The indigenous people of the Andes have a ritual called *pampachanakuy*, where former perpetrators and victims agree to forget aspects of the past. We're talking horrific stuff here – massacres, mass rape, cannibalism. But they know something that we in the West don't know with our 'more truth equals more healing equals more reconciliation' mantra – that a statute of limitations on past crimes is just as important for the *victims* . . .

Mercy   How can I look Angela in the eye and just tell her to forget?

Ben   One bird with broken wings. Thirty-seven thousand, four hundred and fifty-one candidates.

Mercy   Do you know who he is?

Ben   Who?

Mercy   The rapist.

Ben   No! Why would I know that?

Mercy   He was a visiting teacher who came once a week to teach their best students. They've blacked out his professional affiliation, but Juilliard staff teach at the Performing Arts High School –

Ben   And at the special music school, and at Horace Mann, and at Stuyvesant and even all the way up to Connecticut. I didn't keep track of all my colleagues' side hustles for money.

Mercy   But were there rumours?

Ben   There're always rumours. It's every teacher's nightmare. You work so hard to awake a spark of desire – for beauty, for understanding – and you find yourself with something like fatal attraction. Students get close to inspiring teachers. We shouldn't always criminalize desire.

Mercy   I walk through Copley Place every Sunday on the way to church. Where the Pradas and the Armanis and the Alexander McQueens of the world spend millions, millions to awaken desire – for goods I'd never be able to afford. And if I acted on my desire it'd be called shoplifting, or burglary; in the nineteenth century I'd have ended up in a penal colony, in the eighteenth century executed –

Ben   Point taken. But, Mercy – don't underestimate how much pressure a gorgeous young girl –

Mercy   She's a schoolgirl.

Ben   Yeah. They're the worst. Tsunami waves of hormones, amoral, egocentric, flinging themselves kamikaze fashion at any available –

Mercy   Angela's not like that.

Ben   Oh really? Look at this. (*Indicating the report.*) There were four alleged incidents. If it was rape, why didn't she call for help after the first one?

Mercy   Imagine you were a foreigner, or a woman of colour, would you automatically look to the police for help?

Ben   She didn't call the police. She called a child-abuse hotline. I have a friend who volunteers at the Samaritans. Do you know how many pervs they get who just call to masturbate? And slumber-party pranksters – desperate sounding twelve-year-olds who go on and on about the horrific abuse they're suffering – except it ends with giggles and laughter and a sudden hang-up! Ten per cent of the calls to the Ebola hotline in Liberia were pranks! This Angela Chan was twenty flight hours away from home. Probably a bit socially inept like so many of these Asian prodigies. New kid on the block, and she wanted some human sympathy and attention – don't we all? So she made up this whole story, just for a half-hour's temporary intimacy with some phone counsellor, never dreaming it'd be reported to the police and traced back to her.

Birch *enters.*

Ben   Oh hi, Birch.

Pause as **Birch** *surveys the scene.*

Ben   Mercy here went ahead and requested some extracurricular reading.

Mercy   The Angela Chan case.

Birch   Your FOI request?

Mercy   As per our previous discussion. The police report, and the transcripts of the hearing.

Ben (*turning to the back of the file*)   Hang on. Did you see this? She wore Opium.

Birch.   At the hearing?

Ben   These are extracts from her diary.

Mercy   Stop!

Ben   You requested these records, Mercy.

Mercy *grabs hold of the folder and shows* **Ben** *and* **Birch** *a photo of* **Angela**'s *diary.*

Mercy   This is her diary. Her pink Hello Kitty diary with a little heart-shaped lock.

Birch   Goodness.

Mercy *turns another page and shows them scanned pages from* **Angela**'s *diary. The purple inked writing is in Chinese.*

Mercy   Probably written with a scented felt pen. This is a young girl's diary! You can't just read it! It's such a violation . . .

Ben   This is evidence. It's in the public domain.

Mercy   They were translated by a Chinese teacher. A colleague of the rapist's. Does that sound like an impartial translation to you, Birch? It's misleading! Ripped out of context!

Birch   How do you know?

Mercy   Angela told me.

Birch   Do you have independent verification of the translator's identity? Have you consulted a Chinese speaker on the accuracy of the translations?

Mercy   They were plastered all over the school e-bulletin board! Tell me that's not an inside job.

Ben (*reads*)   'Today I have a private lesson with "blank". I spray Opium by YSL on my hair, my throat, my cleavage, my thighs. I wear my Victoria Secrets black-lace bra and panties and spray them too.' That's just classic – Opium! Casts Little Miss China-Doll in a whole different light, doesn't it?

Mercy   It's just perfume! Birch. The judge appointed for the hearing was a Performing Arts High School alumnus. He used the 'beyond all reasonable doubt' rather than 'preponderance of evidence' standard to judge the allegations. What do you think of that?

Birch (*beat*)   I think it sounds like some basic errors were made.

Mercy   Angela did not have her own lawyer. The school used a top law firm to conduct the investigation.

Birch (*beat*)   That does seem to suggest something rather more than incompetence.

Ben   'For my birthday, I wore my DKNY T-shirt with the plunging neckline . . . seventeen cupcakes from Lulu's . . . We played the "Ave Maria" together. Every time I gave the cue, I leaned over so he could see down my shirt. Maybe he likes-*likes* me, as a man desires a woman?' How does that sound to you, Birch?

Birch   I wouldn't read too much into that. Girls use their diaries to fantasize all the time.

Mercy   I certainly did.

Ben   'I wish I were a little African girl. I wish my body had been purged by FGM, that my sinful desiring part had been cut out of me when I was seven.' She felt pleasure. Then the guilt came crashing down. It was buyer's remorse. Not rape.

Birch   Even if she writhed around naked on his knee, he was still duty bound to restrain himself.

Scene Eight

February.

The admissions office.

Angela *knocks and enters without waiting for a reply.*

Angela   Hi, Mercy!

Mercy   Angela. I would appreciate it if you made an appointment first.

Angela   I emailed.

Mercy   It must have gone into spam. What can I do for you?

Angela   I borrowed a violin, and played the blues busker piece! I haven't been able to play since – you know . . .

Mercy   I'm very happy for you.

Angela   It's all because of you – it's the violinist, not the violin. Thank you so much.

Mercy   You've very welcome. Now if you'd excuse me –

Angela   But I still can't play my Bach aria.

Mercy   Which Bach aria?

Angela   My competition aria. The 'Have Mercy Upon Me' aria.

Mercy   Why don't you just change your piece to a Paganini or something.

Angela   I can't.

Mercy   You can change it once.

Angela   This Bach aria is like a mountain in my path. There's no way around it. I have to scale it. But every time I even think about playing it, I hear the violin part in an impossibly high register, mocking me, crushing me –

Mercy   Why don't you get professional help –

Angela   It's what I heard when he forced me on my knees.

Mercy   Stop.

Angela   When he grabbed my hair, when he pushed me down, when he undid his zip, the *stench*, the suffocation –

Mercy   You wanted it.

Angela   No.

Mercy   Don't lie to me, stop lying to me –

Angela   I'm telling the truth!

Mercy   You wanted the sinful desiring part cut out of your body.

Angela   You read my diary?

Mercy   How dare you trivialize, *appropriate* female genital mutilation for some sick rape fantasy!

Angela   No!

Mercy   Did you feel pleasure? Yes or no?

Angela   I hate him!

Mercy   Yes or no.

Angela   I was so scared, he stank, it was gross, but he *forced* me to *feel . . . against my will* you've got to understand, he prided himself on – he did things to me – I can't even describe – his stubble like rough towels rubbing against my thighs – my body did things and felt things I could not stop –

Mercy   It's not tickling. A woman needs to feel some emotional – to feel safe. Loved. No one can force you to have an orgasm.

Angela   How would you know?

Mercy   You're reviving every cliché about women and rape – 'her lips say no but her cunt says yes' – You don't deserve the title of 'rape survivor'.

Angela   I never used that word. Good rape victims only feel pain and revulsion. That's why I'd never press charges though I hate him, I hate him, I hate him for what he did, I hate it that he did whatever he wanted to my body, I hate that I let him do it, I hate it most that my body responded.

Mercy   Shouldn't have seduced him at your little cupcake party then.

Angela   Cupcakes?

Mercy   From Lulu's.

Angela   He got the cupcakes. For my seventeenth birthday.

Mercy   You let him look down your shirt!

Angela   And I have paid. He shoved it up my butt that last time. I thought I was going to split in half, like the magician sawing the woman in two but for real. He came. I curled up in a ball. He went down on me, and I came and came and came. After that, for two weeks, every time I took a step, I felt such pain, but the pain made me want to come again. I know I've become a monster. My wires are twisted between pleasure and pain, love and hate. I'll never get married, have kids, be normal.

Pause.

Mercy (*slowly*)   Your seventeenth birthday. How long had he been teaching you when you turned seventeen?

Angela   Four months.

Mercy   The age of consent is seventeen in New York State. Sex with a minor under seventeen is statutory rape.

Pause.

Angela   He waited until I turned seventeen.

Scene Nine

The lights dim. Voices representing alumni who report on their achievements, their failures and their disorientation.

A   We welcomed Carol Sibyl Blair to the world today. Her parents and four Eliot godparents are very proud!

B   Currently interning in China with the Nature Conservancy in Sichuan. Looking forward to a future that is as multilingual, multicultural and spicy as my present!

C   Appointed Senior Vice President at the World Bank.

D   I am now a federal judge in Massachusetts.

A   After ten years in management consulting, I teach roller-blading in Central Park.

B   I'm thirty-five and still wondering what to do when I grow up.

C   I write to you from federal prison. I've been here since last October for mis-selling municipal bonds. Tutoring prisoners in English and statistics.

D   Ex-Lehman Brothers banker, driving an ice-cream van in New Jersey.

A   Current occupation – prisoner. Achievements – eight life sentences. Current address: No. 04475-046, US Penitentiary – Max –

This scene overlaps with . . .

Scene Ten

March.

Admissions office.

Birch *stands facing the audience.* **Ben** *and* **Mercy** *are seated with the audience.*

Birch (*reading from the alumni magazine, simultaneously with* **B** *from the last scene*)   'Current occupation – prisoner. Achievements – eight life sentences. Current address: No. 04475-046, US Penitentiary – Max.' (*Beat.*) Acceptance by Eliot is not a golden ticket to Willy Wonka's Chocolate Factory, it would seem. (*Beat.*) I know passions are running high. I know that the thirty cases we will discuss in full committee today have their champions and their detractors. I know there will be a desperate scrambling for the last five places. But let's remember we're not God. We are not Fate. And we will get some of it wrong. We think we're judging these young people, but perhaps it is we who are being judged. As individuals. As an institution. Mercy, if you would present the first case, Angela Chan –

Mercy *doesn't stir.*

Birch   Mercy – your floor.

Mercy   I have nothing to add.

Birch (*beat*)   Very well then. Let's vote. Yays – ten – (*Puts up her hand.*) Nays.

Ben*'s hand shoots up.*

Birch   Eleven. Abstentions: fourteen. Mercy – is that an abstention?

Pause. **Mercy** *puts up her hand tentatively.*

Birch   Fifteen. Unless Angela Chan wins the music-scholarship competition next week, she is a rejection.

Scene Eleven

April. Afternoon.

Admissions office.

Birch   We can't possibly afford two air tickets plus accommodation for every accepted candidate.

Ben   These families believe Eliot to be an alien, hostile world. We've got to show them their kids are welcome, that they can *belong*. We're talking – how many here? Fifty possible candidates from rough inner-city neighbourhoods, and another fifty from Arkansas, Alabama, the Appalachian states –

Mercy   Redneck country. Breitbart country.

Ben   Class diversity is just as important as racial diversity, Mercy. So two hundred air tickets. Eliot can afford two hundred air tickets to fly in diverse candidates and their parents, and we're going to lay it on for them. I want the parents put up in the Eliot guest house. I want each candidate to be paired up with a student from a similar background. I want each family to get a free Boston City pass. I want the families to feel like we really want them here as well, that we're not going to take their sons and daughters and turn them into unrecognizable snobs after four years.

Birch   We don't have the budget for it. I'm sorry.

Ben   Yale's doing it. Stanford's doing it. Princeton is flying out both parents of the candidates they most want.

Birch   We can continue this discussion later. Shall we?

Ben   What?

Birch   It's almost time for the music-scholarship competition.

Ben   Afraid I'm going to have to take a rain-check.

Birch   You're a music professor.

Ben   And I've got to call the mother of a Black jazz pianist in Baltimore. She doesn't think we're offering her daughter enough financial aid.

Ben *exits.*

Birch   Mercy?

Mercy   I'm meeting with a Native American lacrosse player.

Knocking at the door.

Birch *answers the door.*

Angela *is at the door with her violin. She is wearing a blue evening dress.*

Birch   Oh hello, Angela.

Angela   Good afternoon, Dr Coffin.

Mercy *packs up her stuff and leaves.*

Birch   The competition is in Paine Hall.

Angela *enters. She catches a glimpse of the departing* **Mercy**.

Angela   I'm not playing.

Birch   Are you still struggling to play?

Angela   No. I choose not to play.

Birch (*beat*)   Just to be clear – you will be forfeiting your last chance of getting into Eliot.

Angela   I've been accepted at Yale and Stanford.

Birch   But did you get enough financial aid from them?

Pause. The answer is no.

Angela, you could forfeit any possibility of staying on in this country

Angela (*derisively*)   'Life, liberty and the pursuit of happiness'?

Birch   So what will you do?

Angela   You think I can't just walk away from it all?

Birch   You have come dressed to play. (*Beat.*) Very well then. I shall go and withdraw your name from the competition.

Birch *moves towards the exit.*

Angela   How does the 'Mercy' aria start? With a violin solo too high for the human voice to reach, phrases too long for human lungs to sustain, ornamentation too intricate . . . The singer tries so hard to copy the melody but can't. It's mocking, it's derisive, it's crushing . . .

Birch   But the violin solo is propelled by that 12/8 walking bass – those tears flowing down Peter's cheeks. That divine glory is not indifferent to our pain.

Angela   In Hong Kong I was a Ming vase, mute, polished, ornamental, but there was an honesty to that. No one ever said I was a great artiste, a unique talent; no one took my hand and promised me the keys to paradise.

Beat.

Do you know what Bach did with his music? His boy choristers sang his *Matthew Passion* to condemned criminals en route to the gallows. He stood me up against the back of a sofa and made me play Bach. I played with all my heart, with all my strength; I prayed for a miracle – for an angel with flaming sword to stop him . . . but all the angel did was crush me . . .

Birch   So play that.

Angela   What?

Birch   Play it angry. Ugly. Broken.

Angela   How can I possibly play anything after this? There's nothing left. I could play at Carnegie Hall, I could play with the Berlin Philharmonic, I could win Grammy Awards and at the end of the day still just be a body to be used by men, abused by men. You know and I know that's what the world sees when it sees me. (*Beat.*) Isn't that what you see?

Birch   No. I bet that if you play, you'll find you've not been abandoned. That broken voice – isn't it absolutely supported from above and below? That violin solo is a promise that even at the breaking point, when you feel utterly abandoned, utterly alone, there's always someone to accompany you on your path. When your breath runs out, when your song's about to die, there's a violin there to catch you and complete the song.

Both **Angela** *and* **Birch** *hear the 'Mercy' aria in its full glory – (bars 15–23, the violin/voice duet).*

Scene Twelve

May.

Birch *is packing up the contents of her desk into boxes.*

Mercy *enters.*

Pause.

Mercy   I still don't understand why you are leaving. Why now? There's so much to do, so many pieces to pick up – the new guidelines on mental health, the new sexual-harassment procedures . . . What will you do?

Birch   Thirty years ago, my father forbade me the study of theology because he thought women couldn't be clergy. I am enrolling at Yale Divinity School. (*Beat.*) I hope you are staying. Good luck.

Birch *has finished packing and puts on her light spring coat.*

Mercy   I just felt she needed a fresh start.

Birch   Who?

Mercy   Angela Chan. (*Beat.*) Manchester is a great city. (*Beat.*) We don't really have the resources to support someone so traumatized . . . (*Beat.*) She played like she was at war – she's obviously deeply disturbed. I'm surprised she got second. That was – whatever that was, it wasn't Bach.

Birch   You were there?

Mercy   I sneaked in. I was at the back. Just couldn't stay away.

Pause.

Ben *enters.*

Ben   Birch! I just want to say – thank you so much for all you've done here. Whatever I go on to achieve in this role, I'm very much aware it's because I stand on the shoulders of a giant.

Birch   Thank you.

Birch *leaves.*

Ben *goes to his desk, and takes out a bottle of champagne and two glasses. He pours and hands* **Mercy** *a glass.*

Ben   Cheers!

Ben *drains a glass.*

Mercy   Are you drinking to Birch's resignation?

Ben   I've just spoken to our lawyers – you're permanent now. The visa too.

Mercy   Thank you.

Ben   Where would I be without my right-hand woman? What's wrong?

Mercy   Nothing. I just have a migraine.

Ben (*moving closer*)   Acupressure?

Mercy (*backing away*)   I just need to lie down in a dark room. (*Beat.*) How did you know she was gorgeous?

Ben   What?

Mercy   Angela Chan. You said don't underestimate the pressure a gorgeous young girl can put on a man. How did you know she was gorgeous?

Ben   You told me.

Mercy   No I didn't.

Ben   Birch must have told me. What does it matter anyway.

Pause.

Mercy   See you tomorrow, Professor Cohen . . . Dean Cohen.

Scene Thirteen

Fifteen months ago.

Foyer of Lincoln Center, New York City.

Angela *is in a blue evening dress. She has her violin with her. She's lining up at the bar.*

Ben *enters and stands next to* **Angela**.

Ben   Chocolate or vanilla?

Angela   I'm sorry?

Ben   Do you like chocolate ice cream, or vanilla? Or perhaps you like raspberry sorbet –

Angela   Green tea.

Ben   The line for hot beverages is over there.

Angela   I like green-tea ice cream.

Ben   Why not. There I am, the blundering American –

Angela   No worries.

Ben   Schubert or Schumann?

Angela   What?

Ben   Would you prefer to meet Schubert or Schumann – say at a bar?

Angela   Schumann was insane. Schubert had syphilis. Definitely Schumann.

They laugh.

Ben   I like that. Who's your favourite Muppet?

Angela   Kermit.

Ben   The voice of idealism. With a sense of irony. Have you seen the Kermit Klein ads?

Angela   No.

Ben   Oh they're utterly hilarious. You've seen those Calvin Klein ads with Marky Mark?

Angela   Yes . . .

Ben   Kermit Klein is a spoof.

Angela   So a moodily lit Kermit –

Ben   Black and white, very classy –

Angela   With his briefs sticking out of his jeans?

Ben   You bet.

Angela   Miss Piggy must be delighted –

Ben   Yup. No prizes for guessing what she's doing in her panties – ah sorry, sorry. Look I don't think they've quite caught up to green-tea ice cream here. Can I get you strawberry?

Angela   No I'm fine. Thanks.

Ben   A drink? Oooh look at this, a green-tea mojito!

Angela   I don't have ID.

Ben (*mock-grandiosely*)   She's with me. Cocktail for the lady, please. On the rocks.

Angela *giggles.*

Angela   I don't think we have time before the second half begins.

Ben   Do we have to go back in?

Angela   I felt very – disturbed too. Midori plays like she's at war –

Ben   Don't blame you. I remember when Midori was a dainty Japanese elf of a child prodigy. She's really let herself go.

Angela   You don't worry about your looks when you're struggling with the angel.

Ben   You've lost me there.

Angela   She plays Bach like it's a dark labyrinth, concealing a divinity in its heart.

Ben   I'd love to hear you play.

Angela   I could be terrible.

Ben   I doubt it.

A bell rings. The PA system announces that the concert will commence again in five minutes.

Angela *gets up.*

Ben   Say we have fifty grand to consume tonight – *consume*, all of it, tonight, so no buying of property, no investment, no giving away to charity – what would you do?

Angela   That's easy.

Ben   You think?

Angela   I would hire Carnegie Hall, and the Gibson Stradivarius –

Ben   The one stolen from the dressing room of Carnegie Hall?

Angela   Then sold to a hack musician who played it in restaurants for the next fifty years. No one noticed.

Ben   The thief confesses on his deathbed, and Joshua Bell buys the Strad.

Angela   He busks like a hobo in the Washington metro –

Ben   A superstar violinist, playing Bach on a Stradivarius during morning rush hour –

Angela   Seven people stopped –

Ben   Thirty-two dollars in tips. A total flop!

Angela   Do you really think so? You never know who receives the music. And seven people stopped.

Ben   I love your passion. (*Beat.*) So what would you do once you have this incognito Stradivarius in Carnegie Hall? I can see you there, charming the pants off everyone, cameras lapping you up, glowing alabaster in your blue dress, like a Ming vase –

Angela   It's not Ming blue.

Ben   It's a lovely shade –

Angela   It's ultramarine.

Ben   Aha! A fan of Renaissance painting –

Angela   Rembrandt.

Ben (*confused*)   A Rembrandt blue?

Angela   There is no blue in Rembrandt.

Ben (*beat*)   You're right. He doesn't really venture beyond yellow in the colour spectrum. I never noticed. Why?

Angela   There is no heaven in Rembrandt.

Ben   There is no heaven in Rembrandt. Fascinating. You have a beautiful mind. I usually try to make MetFridays. Any chance of seeing you there?

Angela   What's MetFridays?

Ben   The Metropolitan Museum of Art is open late every Friday evening. You from out of town?

Angela (*embarrassed*)   No. Yes. I just got here.

Ben   From where?

Angela   Hong Kong.

Ben   Wow. Fresh off the plane!

Angela   You think I'm provincial?

Ben   Not at all. You're passionate and sophisticated and – ultramarine – that's the colour of the Virgin Mary, isn't it?

Angela   Yes.

A moment.

Ben   And what brings you to New York City?

Angela   I got a scholarship to the Performing Arts High School.

Ben   I teach there once a week! (*Beat.*) So I will get to hear you play . . .

Pause.

The bell rings, summoning the audience.

What's your name?

Angela   Angela.

The End.

Learning Pack by Amy Ng (Author)

On re-reading Acceptance *to prepare for this learning resource package, I was surprised and delighted to discover that the play felt more resonant than ever before.*
– AMY NG

Contents

Quotes from an exclusive interview with the playwright Amy Ng are featured throughout the learning pack.

Learning Pack Introduction by Amy Ng

I was born in Australia, grew up in Hong Kong, lived in the United States, Germany, Austria and Japan, and am now based in the United Kingdom. I trained as a historian, with research interests in multinational empires, imperial decline and nationality conflict, and am the author of *Nationalism and Political Liberty*. I am fluent in English, German and Chinese and regularly translate contemporary Chinese plays into English.

I am a political playwright.

But what exactly is a political playwright?

Even when my plays are not about Politics with a capital P, they are always about how big political issues are refracted in individual lives. There is a venerable tradition of agitprop theatre, where the plays are written to promote a certain political viewpoint, party, or programme. However, I feel my role is akin to that of the child in 'The Emperor's New Clothes'. The child does not call for constitutional limits on the Emperor's powers, or the overthrow of the monarchy, or the establishment of a socialist republic. The child points out that the emperor is naked. Similarly, I believe that in a society based on ideological blinkers, propaganda and outright lies, the first step is to speak truth to power.

There is another kind of political play which emphasizes trauma and atrocities, with the goal of calling out the (usually white) mainstream audience, as well as affirming the experiences of minority communities – 'we hear you, we see you, these things happened and they are important'. While both goals are vitally important, I feel that an exclusive focus on victimization risks making the victims passive. I write from the agency of the survivors, the way they resist, fight back and heal, and therefore I write from hope.

My activism as a political playwright lies in empowerment, by exploring the possibility of agency even in the bleakest situation.

I wrote Acceptance *at the same time as writing my first play, I was writing both plays in parallel, so it was simply a matter of which play was going to be picked first. I started writing* Acceptance *in 2014 and it was staged in 2018 – it just shows how long this process can take.*
– AMY NG

The Play

Angela Chan from Hong Kong is a prodigy. A brilliant student, a world-class musician, she's the perfect candidate, except for a controversy she cannot escape.

Mercy Jones is a Black British feminist – driven, honest and totally committed to achieving a level playing field for people of colour.

Both have their eye on the prize – America's elite Eliot University. But Angela was raped by her music tutor and her allegations were rejected. Is she a victim or a liar? When Mercy, the newly appointed diversity expert at Eliot, takes up Angela's case to be accepted into Eliot, she unleashes a tornado in the oak-panelled corridors as attitudes and agendas are exposed . . .

Settings

The setting is the admissions office of an Ivy League university in Boston – in other words, a passionately contested field where idealism and social engineering collide with financial constraints and the interests of alumni and donors.

The composition of the student body at elite universities directly impacts on the composition of future societal elites, which means that what happens in a university admissions office has implications for the whole of society.

Time

Set in the present, the action covers one academic year, from October to May.

Champions of Activism Challenge: Gain knowledge, so you can impart knowledge . . .

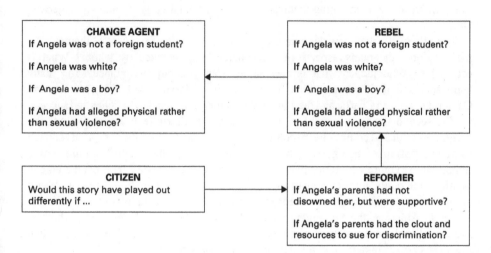

CHANGE AGENT

If Angela was not a foreign student?

If Angela was white?

If Angela was a boy?

If Angela had alleged physical rather than sexual violence?

REBEL

If Angela was not a foreign student?

If Angela was white?

If Angela was a boy?

If Angela had alleged physical rather than sexual violence?

CITIZEN

Would this story have played out differently if ...

REFORMER

If Angela's parents had not disowned her, but were supportive?

If Angela's parents had the clout and resources to sue for discrimination?

Themes

The play has three overarching themes: acceptance, sexual violation and the American Dream.

The title of the play was deliberately chosen as it is one of the central themes. The play explores the many aspects of 'acceptance' – acceptance by whom? What is acceptable? Who judges what is acceptable? Can you buy acceptance? Too many applicants and their parents think acceptance into Harvard and Yale, Oxford and Cambridge is like a Charlie and the Chocolate Factory golden ticket to riches and success.

The second theme of sexual violation – and the after-effects which include the feelings of guilt and complicity, becoming an outcast, post-traumatic symptoms and the re-traumatization of being publicly judged in a 'blame the victim' culture – was important to explore within this play as it was based on a real story. This enabled me to highlight the public implications of rape – specifically why allegations of sexual abuse arouse so much ambivalence and fear in individuals as well as in institutions.

Set in America, the attainment of the American Dream as something which is available for all hard-working migrants is questioned in this play. Moreover, how that dream is so often undermined by xenophobia, racism and sexism.

But, most importantly, my play is about hope and self-acceptance. The play ends with Angela finding her 'America' within herself rather than outside in a foreign country.

The Writing Process

Acceptance grew out of the real life experience of a Hong Kong student who went for an admissions interview at an Ivy League University, where she was interrogated about her sexual harassment allegations against her boarding school teacher.

The very first scene I wrote was Scene Two, which is close to being a verbatim account of the admissions interview. The student expected to be discussing her academic and extra-curricular activities, future goals, etc., only to be cross-examined instead about the sexual assault allegations which she had thought confidential.

In its first iteration, the play happened in two time frames – seventeen-year-old Angela and the thirty-year-old Mercy bonding and clashing in the late nineties, then meeting up again fifteen years later, which gave the play a sense of reckoning with a live, traumatic past.

Acceptance was workshopped for a week in 2015, followed by a rehearsed reading at the Vibrant Festival, Finborough Theatre, by which time I had rewritten the entire action to be set in the present, feeling that a pressure-cooker play would better serve the urgency of the themes than a multi-timeline play.

It was picked up by Hampstead Theatre in the summer of 2017, and programmed for March 2018. In the meantime, #metoo broke out in 2017 and sparked a new movement worldwide, holding powerful men to account. This inevitably influenced the writing and production of the play.

At the beginning, I thought of the play as an ensemble piece comprising various admissions officers, all with very different agendas, as they deliberate Angela's case. However, I felt after a couple of drafts that this inadvertently silenced the victim all over again. Moreover, the public aspects of rape – the reputational damage, the judgement by strangers – could not really be explored separately from the painful internal process of healing.

Initially, I wanted Angela to be judged by strangers, to highlight how the issues of power raised by sexual assault allegations, gender stereotypes and discomfort around sexuality can drive people to extreme judgements on people they have never met. In previous drafts, none of the admissions officers knew Angela prior to the application process. However, to increase the dramatic tension of the play, and probably under the influence of #metoo and the calling out of powerful men, I made Ben into the villain of the piece.

Since *Acceptance* was to receive its world premiere in London, we explored the possibility of relocating the action to the United Kingdom. However, *Acceptance* is set specifically in an admissions office already embroiled in heated debates about sexual harassment and violence as well as diversity and inclusion in education. At the time of writing, both issues did not loom large in the British public consciousness, though this has since changed.

Practical Challenge: First bell

Pick a character from the play then select a scene featuring that character

Perform that scene once as a cold read. Then perform it again immediately.

Make a note of the character decisions you made instinctually.

What kind of person was your character?

Read your chosen scene again, then use the scenarios below to develop your character and then act out a scene embodying them

What is the song that changed your character's life? What was your character's situation before they heard/engaged with 'their' song? Where did the song take them? What changed in their life after hearing the song?

What does the song mean to your character at different stages in their life?

- *At age twelve*
- *At age fifteen*
- *At age eighteen*
- *When they first kissed someone*
- *When they first broke up with someone*
- *The first time they witnessed someone's death*

There was once a woman with a burning secret that she absolutely could not tell anyone, but threatened to consume her if she didn't let it out. One day she climbed a mountain and discovered a tree with a hole in the shape of a human ear. She whispered her secret into the tree.

What secret would your character whisper into the 'listening tree'?

Your character has $50,000 they can spend tonight. They have to spend it on themselves; they cannot save it up, or give it away to charity, or invest it. What would they do?

Your character is dead. They can carry one memory with them into the afterlife. What would that memory be?

Afterwards, discuss as a group how the decisions you made as the character influenced the actions and choices made in the scene

- How did it influence the way your character moved around the space?
- How did it influence your character's physicality?
- How did it influence your character's relationship with other characters?

- Was your character perceived by others as you intended?
- What did you add to ensure your character was three-dimensional and was a fully fledged person with nuance?
- What small changes could you have made to your character that would alter them fundamentally?

Champions of Activism Challenge: Step out of your comfort zone and make it your own . . .

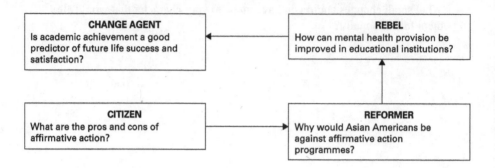

CHANGE AGENT
Is academic achievement a good predictor of future life success and satisfaction?

REBEL
How can mental health provision be improved in educational institutions?

CITIZEN
What are the pros and cons of affirmative action?

REFORMER
Why would Asian Americans be against affirmative action programmes?

This play is based on a real story of a student from Hong Kong who went to Boarding school and later interviewed at Harvard University in America in the 1990s. I've been carrying this story around with me since then, knowing that I would write about it one day – but not knowing what form it would take.
It's always about finding the agency of the victims. That is where the hope is. Perpetrators try to take away your agency, so you really should not do that as a writer.
– AMY NG

Practical Challenge: Assembly

On the *Beyond The Canon's Plays for Young Activists'* supporting website you will find my answers to the character questionnaire that I did for Angela in 2015.

Read them carefully, then act out your scene from the 'first bell' challenge again, this time using my answers to develop your character.

As a group discuss the scene

How did the scene alter when you did it without any character development work?

What felt like the more comfortable performance?

How did it alter how your character related to the other characters?

How did it alter your character's physicality?

Which process did you find easier? The provocations, the Character Questionnaire or when you did neither?

Champions of Activism Challenge: Your agency is your superpower! How will you use it . . .?

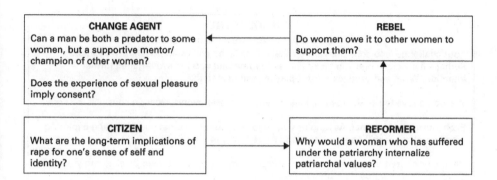

CHANGE AGENT

Can a man be both a predator to some women, but a supportive mentor/ champion of other women?

Does the experience of sexual pleasure imply consent?

REBEL

Do women owe it to other women to support them?

CITIZEN

What are the long-term implications of rape for one's sense of self and identity?

REFORMER

Why would a woman who has suffered under the patriarchy internalize patriarchal values?

Champions of Activism Challenge: Now, change the world for the better and create something new

---

CHANGE AGENT

Congratulations! You are a Change Agent!

Your challenge is to consider various challenges faced by young people in education. Perhaps it's a challenge you faced yourself or one that you believe requires further attention. Write and produce a short play in response to this.

We would love to see the results. Please send to info@beyondthecanon.com

Each journey is personal. As long as you keep expanding on what you know and exploring what you don't, it will be easier to stand more firmly in your truth.

We are honoured to have been a part of your journey and will forever be cheering you on. Onwards and upwards, Champion of Activism!

Where Next?

Amy Ng published plays

Acceptance

Shangri-La

British East Asian Plays edited by Lucy Chau Lai-Tuen and Cheryl Robson
Published by Aurora Metro Books (2018)
First collection of full-length plays from British East Asian Playwrights. Features:
Special Occasions by Amy Ng.

Recommended plays that address similar themes to *Acceptance* by playwrights from the global majority

Guillermo Calderón, *Villa*
Anupama Chandrasekhar, *When the Crows Visit*
Makrand Deshpande, *Balatkar Please Stop It!*
Rajiv Joseph, *The North Pool*
Yaël Farber, *Nirbhaya*
Dominique Morisseau, *Pipeline*
Tarell Alvin McCraney, *Choir Boy*
Mallika Taneja and Shena Gamat, *Allegedly*
Naomi Wallace, *The Breach*
Zhang Xian, *Rape*